Intellectual Creativity in First-Year Composition Classes

Intellectual Creativity in First-Year Composition Classes

Building a Case for the Multigenre Research Project

Heidi Wall Burns and Michael MacBride

ROWMAN & LITTLEFIELD
Lanham • Boulder • New York • London

Published by Rowman & Littlefield
A wholly owned subsidiary of The Rowman & Littlefield Publishing Group, Inc.
4501 Forbes Boulevard, Suite 200, Lanham, Maryland 20706
www.rowman.com

Unit A, Whitacre Mews, 26-34 Stannary Street, London SE11 4AB

Copyright © 2016 by Heidi Wall Burns and Michael MacBride

All rights reserved. No part of this book may be reproduced in any form or by any electronic or mechanical means, including information storage and retrieval systems, without written permission from the publisher, except by a reviewer who may quote passages in a review.

British Library Cataloguing in Publication Information Available

Library of Congress Cataloging-in-Publication Data Available
ISBN 978-1-4758-2492-6 (cloth : alk. paper)
ISBN 978-1-4758-2496-4 (pbk. : alk. paper)
ISBN 978-1-4758-2497-1 (electronic)

∞™ The paper used in this publication meets the minimum requirements of American National Standard for Information Sciences—Permanence of Paper for Printed Library Materials, ANSI/NISO Z39.48-1992.

Printed in the United States of America

Contents

Acknowledgments vii

Foreword ix

1 **Justification of the MGRP in the Freshman Composition Classroom** 1

2 **The Self-Contained Unit for the MGRP** 15

3 **The Whole Semester Adaptation of the MGRP** 39

4 **Plug-In Activities** 55
   Introduction 55
   Plug-In Activity 1: Analyzing Genre: Using Newspapers in the Classroom 57
   Plug-In Activity 2: Audience Awareness Activity: Let's Raise That Tuition! 60
   Plug-In Activity 3: Evaluating Websites for Source Material: Is It CRAAP or Crap? 63
   Plug-In Activity 4: Teaching Students about Genre: Writing about the Weather 66
   Plug-In Activity 5: Writing a "How-To": Teaching the Process Genre 68
   Plug-In Activity 6: Infographic Making 71
   Plug-In Activity 7: Library Scavenger Hunt 74
   Plug-In Activity 8: Practicing Research Skills: APA Library Research 77
   Plug-In Activity 9: Summarizing Using Stories 80

5 **Assessment and Evaluation** 83

Appendix A: Assignment Sheet for MGRP Self-Contained Unit ... 97
Appendix B: MGRP Topic Proposal Handout for Self-Contained Unit ... 99
Appendix C: Assignment Sheet for Whole Semester Adaptation ... 101
Appendix D: Assignment Sheet for Assignment #1: Overview/Summary/Background ... 105
Appendix E: Workshop for Assignment #1: MGRP Self-Contained Unit ... 107
Appendix F: Checklist for Workshop Day ... 109
Appendix G: Assignment Sheet for Assignment #2: Annotated Bibliography ... 113
Appendix H: Assignment Sheet for Assignment #3: Self-Reflection ... 115
Appendix I: Final Workshop for MGRP Self-Contained Unit ... 117
Appendix J: List of Former Student Topics ... 121
Appendix K: Formal Submission Expectations for MGRP Self-contained Unit ... 123
Appendix L: MGRP Grading Rubric for Whole Semester Assignment ... 125
Appendix M: MGRP Grading Rubric for Self-Contained Unit ... 127
Appendix N: List of Potential Genres ... 131
Bibliography ... 133
Index ... 139
About the Authors ... 143

Acknowledgments

Heidi thanks her husband Matt, and her three boys, Joe, Sean, and Aidan, for their encouragement to try new things and their patience as she worked late into the night. Without their support, this project would have never come to fruition. Also, special thanks to her co-author Michael who enthusiastically embraced this crazy project early on and never looked back. It's been a pleasure.

Michael thanks his wife (Gayle) and two boys (Dylan and Parker) for both giving him space and happy distractions during the writing process. He also thanks his co-author, Heidi, for believing in the project and for being an amazing person to work with.

Foreword

I remember, many years ago, picking up Tom Romano's *Blending Genre, Altering Style* and devouring it as an early-career teacher. Immediately, I made a space in the high school writing course I was teaching for the multigenre project, because I could see how the writing was more authentic, more organic. Despite some of the suspicious questions from colleagues who asked things like, "do our kids even know what the word *genre* means?" I was determined to break some of the long-held beliefs about what writing in school looks like.

So we collected. We drafted. We embedded our research. The students were engaged, and I was directing it all with what felt like the precision of a conductor's baton. Then a colleague finishing her PhD asked if she could use my classroom as part of her dissertation research on multigenre writing. I was thrilled to share all of our process and products and just as anxious to read her final insights.

Many months later, my dear friend carefully handed me a copy of her dissertation with few words and one cautious invitation, "I'll be interested to know what you think." As I read, I began to understand her hesitancy. Her research revealed what my young teaching self couldn't see: I had fundamentally misunderstood the spirit of multigenre writing. In short, we had been doing multigenre *projects*, but multigenre isn't a project, it's a way of teaching. It isn't a procedure, it's a philosophy.

This insight became a doorway to a fundamental misunderstanding about teaching I was clasping tightly: it's never the things or the tasks that grow our learners, instead, it's the way we nurture them to become *writers*, not students of writing.

This is precisely where *Intellectual Creativity in First-Year Composition Classes: Building a Case for the Multigenre Research Project* situates itself:

that vexing moment when we realize our students may be playing along more than they are constructing their own learning. Like all of us, these authors were confronted with choices: carry on or change. It's not just that they changed, it's what they discovered as they used multigenre approach to liberate their writers. The lessons they offer us go well beyond a paper or project; they're a roadmap for engaging learners in the most crucial ways.

IT'S NOT RESEARCH WRITING, IT'S ABOUT BECOMING *RESEARCHERS*

In the same way I had to learn the tough lesson about the difference between a multigenre writing project and teaching with a multigenre philosophy, these professors are cultivating *researchers*. As educators, it's easy to carry the misunderstanding that the task does the teaching. While it's true that design matters, even the most beautifully conceived assignment can't do the teaching for us.

This is precisely why the shift in both mindset and mantra from "research writing" to "researchers" is imperative. It's the outward expression of an inward philosophy that says *we want our learners to embody the dispositions of researchers, not just complete an assignment*. It says *we know that researchers must be discerning and thoughtful, careful, and consistent*. It says *we understand bringing multigenre writing into our curriculums may cause some uneasiness in the unknown, but it's only through struggle that our writers will find themselves.*

This transfer, from task to embodiment, is tough for teachers and students alike. It's why we flatten the hierarchies of our classrooms to elevate everyone to the status of learner. So we can eliminate the fear of having to be experts before we teach something new and replace it with curiosity and the willingness to learn alongside each other.

LEARNING HAPPENS WHEN WE TRANSFER

As the authors in this book asked themselves the toughest questions about student engagement, they also happened upon an important truth: transfer is the outward expression of learning. Every time we ask a student to transfer her knowledge or skills to another format, genre, or context, we're asking her to express learning in a new way. Engagement and learning meet in multigenre writing because in order to embed research into authentic genres, writers can't just "stack facts" like I've seen in so many traditional research papers. Rather, they must *engage* in the nuances of genre to embody it. It's a necessary transfer.

As teachers, we can certainly get lulled into the belief that engagement is synonymous with entertainment, especially when we focus on contending with all of the electronic distractions that are rarely beyond a fingertip reach from our students. But it's not true. We *don't* have to entertain our students—we have to challenge them. Choice and authenticity are the roads to engagement, not amusement. As you see the examples of student work unfold throughout this book, you'll see what engagement really looks like: attention to detail, transfer of knowledge, authentic work that goes beyond the context of a school assignment. In short, you'll see engaged learning.

ASKING QUESTIONS INSTEAD OF EXPECTING ANSWERS

Perhaps one of the most important tools any teacher has is the power of the question. But not for the reasons we're most likely to first assume. A question's influence isn't in its tether to an answer; rather, it's in the space of uncertainty it creates for the learner. That "struggle space" to reconcile the unknown, to delve deeper, to practice curiosity is the stuff of becoming an authentic learner. As the students in the pages of this book are prompted to ask authentic research questions as part of their multigenre work, they are creating individualized learning spaces where purpose and research meet.

As learners set their own purpose for research as an extension of the questions they pose, intentionality becomes palpable. With intention these students find more intrinsic reasons to read and write and think and grow. They transcend what I misunderstood in my early days of teaching multigenre writing, because the students have *real* choice in how they construct meaning and become researchers.

Regardless of where you're at in your teaching journey, when you pick up this book, there's something for you. Perhaps you're like me when I first started working with multigenre: nervous of all the possibilities, afraid of giving up control. Perhaps you've tried it before, but now it's been more of a project instead of a way of teaching and you're looking for the bridge. Perhaps you've long been designing these authentic experiences for your students and are looking for a jolt of affirmation and reinvigoration. Perhaps you're all of these.

No matter your place on the continuum, you'll find in these stories of bringing multigenre writing to life in the classroom, a profound sense of camaraderie. You'll nod in acknowledgement as they unveil their struggle. You'll hear yourself breathe "ah-ha" when the authors share insights that match your questions. You'll find yourself being challenged to think about both the biggest picture and the most specific details of instructional design.

And you'll know that what they say is real because it's grounded in actual classroom experience and reinforced through careful research.

You're about to embark on a necessary read. Enjoy!

Sarah Brown Wessling
2010 National Teacher of the Year

Chapter 1

Justification of the MGRP in the Freshman Composition Classroom

Is it possible to engage your students and equip them with the writing skills they will actually use outside the walls of academia? A couple of semesters ago, Heidi Wall Burns, a seasoned first-year composition instructor, was reviewing her student evaluations from the previous semester. The comments and ratings on the Likert scale were, as expected, positive and provided a strong affirmation of her ability to connect with students and presumably teach them something of value. Overall, the student feedback was satisfying to read.

It wasn't until Heidi started to read the students' responses to the question, "What is the most important thing you learned this semester?" that her enthusiasm began to wane. Student after student responded with something along the lines of "I learned how to use APA documentation in my research papers." At first glance, this would be positive, as that is one of the course objectives. However, upon further reflection, Heidi began to feel uneasy. It is extremely valuable to learn how to properly document research; however, no educator would ever claim it to be the most important thing they taught in a first-year composition class.

The student responses nagged at Heidi as she began to put together a new syllabus for the next semester of students. She took some time to really consider the question of "What is the most important thing you learned this semester?" What do today's students need to learn in a first-year composition course to be successful in their academic careers, and more importantly, in their professional careers outside the walls of academia?

If one does a quick search on the Internet for what millennials need in order to be successful in the workplace, the three most commonly noted skills are critical thinking skills, communication skills, and strong research skills. This is consistent across professions. After much reflection, Heidi realized that the question good educators need to ask is, "Am I equipping my students with the writing skills that will help them become successful in academia and beyond?" Indeed, a quick review of the professional world's opinion of recent college graduates indicates that academia is not meeting the needs of today's students for success outside the walls of academia. Lack of strong writing skills is one of the most lamented concerns!

In "Learning about Self and Others through Multigenre Research Projects," Randi Dickson, Jon DeGraff, and Mark Foard (2002) discuss the need for academia to stop teaching writing projects that aren't "aimed at helping students thrive outside academia" (p. 86). Bruce Pirie, author of *Reshaping High School English* agrees. He says, "We should beware of locking students inside the rooms of our own academic histories" (Pirie, 1997, p. 94), meaning, instructors shouldn't keep teaching the same methodology simply because it worked for them when they were students.

Unfortunately, academia is still teaching students how to research and write like it did in the twentieth (dare we say the nineteenth?) century. Most of today's students prefer to do the majority of their research online. Many of them don't think to turn to books for information at all. In fact, according to the Ethnographic Research in Illinois Academic Libraries (ERIAL) project, a large percentage of today's students have never spoken to a librarian and don't see librarians as academic experts (Kolowich, 2011)! Students far prefer the convenience of the Internet. College writing courses must adapt to this new student preference to make research relevant again.

This led us to reconsider the role that research skills play in the syllabus for a first-year composition course. The *purpose* of research has not changed much over the course of education, from Aristotle to today. In 1982, Richard Larson wrote "The 'Research Paper' in the Writing Course: A Non-Form of Writing" in which he outlines the goals of research as:

1. To learn more about a subject;
2. To engage with other scholar's work;
3. To create a new body of work on a subject;
4. To encounter source material that must be interpreted, evaluated, and organized to acquire value from it (Larson, 1982).

Larson (1982) insists that research is an activity and process and not something that is always done for a specific outcome. He states, "We could probably define 'research' generally as the seeking out of information new to the seeker, for a purpose, and we would probably agree that the researcher usually has to interpret, evaluate, and organize that information before it acquires value" (p. 813).

Although Larson's source is clearly dated, the premise that he is putting forth has not changed—research is meant to engage as an activity.

The research paper is an *additional* activity of output that *might* emerge from the research process. Unfortunately, the way college instructors are teaching research and writing to first-year composition students has not changed much since Larson made this claim in 1982. Most instructors are more focused on the formal submission of the research paper than they are with the research process.

Larson (1982) argues that the basic research essay that most first-year writing courses in college teach is "not defensible" (p. 812) and lacks the transferable skills necessary for students to succeed in other courses. Dickson et al. (2002) support Larson's original premise. They write that most writing assignments created to teach research skills are "narrowly defined and can be done by only one assigned method" (Dickson, DeGraff, & Foard, 2002, p. 86).

Additionally, Larson (1982) claims that there is no one type of research essay anyway. Robert Davis and Mark Shadle (2007) echo this sentiment in *Teaching Multiwriting: Researching and Composing with Multiple Genres, Media, Disciplines, and Cultures*. They claim that in practice, most types of writing require some element of evidence from outside sources for credibility. Students, therefore, need the knowledge of locating, analyzing, summarizing, synthesizing, and acknowledging sources that goes well beyond the conventional research-based essay.

If the students in today's college writing classrooms are going to be successful in the workforce, they need to learn what research is, how to perform it effectively, and how to best communicate their findings. Additionally, they need to be able to see writing and research across genres as a transferable skill to other courses and to non-writing intensive professions. Too often, as Charles Bazerman (2007) writes in "Genre and Cognitive Development: Beyond Writing to Learn," there are "smart, accomplished colleagues in other disciplines who have little vocabulary for discussing writing beyond the corrective grammar they learned in high school" (p. 289).

A conventional research-based essay can teach some research skills, but it fails to teach the student how to make the mental connections between what they learned in the process of writing one assignment for an ENG 101 course and transfer the skills to any other course. Ultimately, will they be able to make the connection to the workplace situation? Larson doesn't believe they will. He writes:

> For me, then, very little is gained by speaking about and teaching, as a generic concept, the so-called "research paper." If anything at all is gained, it is only the reminder that responsible writing normally depends on well-planned investigation of data. But much is lost by teaching the research paper in writing courses as a separately designated activity. For by teaching the generic "research paper"

as a separate activity, instructors in writing signal to their students that there is a kind of writing that incorporates the results of research, and there are (by implication) many kinds of writing that do not and need not do so . . . . And frankly, I can't conceive many teachers of English showing these students what they needed to know either. I can't conceive myself, or very many colleagues (other than trained teachers of technical writing) guiding a student toward a report of a scientific laboratory experiment that a teacher of science would find exemplary. (Larson, 1982, pp. 814–815)

MAKING CONNECTIONS OUTSIDE THE FIRST-YEAR COMPOSITION COURSE

Academia is beginning to catch on that students aren't learning to write across genres. WAC, or Writing Across Curriculums, is a curriculum movement that is emerging not only across U.S. institutions of higher learning but also in the K–12 education system with the introduction of STEAM programs (Science, Technology, Engineering, Art, and Math). A core objective of these initiatives is to help students engage in writing intensive activities in classes that aren't traditionally writing intensive in scope.

Students in first-year writing courses often devalue the writing skills they are being taught, because they don't foresee the usability of writing skills in their career paths. Thus, the goal of a WAC or STEAM program is to encourage the cognitive development in writing that students need to make the connections between the need for strong writing skills in places that aren't traditionally considered writing focused. At the beginning of any given semester, only a handful of students are able to make this connection.

To illustrate to her students that all professions require strong writing skills to some degree, Heidi uses the following brainstorming activity in class. She encourages them to consider places where strong writing skills will bring them success. Inevitably, their first responses are that they won't need to write well. In response to this attitude, Heidi encourages the class to make a list of ways writing will be used across a variety of professions that have no obvious writing components. This brief list includes emails of inquiry, cover letters, resumes, job orders, lab reports, grant proposals, inter-office memos, etc.

After students create this initial list, she broadens the conversation to include non-professional places where writing will matter. Typically, the mini-lecture ends with a statement that takes many students by surprise: *Your intelligence will often be judged by the quality of your writing.*

To support this, Heidi pulls up a news article online and displays it on the Smartboard for the class to view. The class quickly reviews the article, and then Heidi scrolls down to the comments section. It doesn't take long for the students to get the point—the well-written comments are taken by and large more seriously than the comments that are rife with grammatical errors or that lack structure. It's a very simple illustration, but it has a profound impact on how the students view the value of competent writing outside of the composition classroom.

The other major dilemma in teaching a conventional research-based essay is the student perception of research and its purpose. In a typical semester, Heidi starts the research unit by conducting another brainstorming activity with her classes. She asks them: "What comes to mind when you hear the word research?" (Note, she does not say research *papers*).

The responses are mostly what she expects. Actual student responses include:

- Time-consuming
- Looking up information about things I don't care about
- Too many open tabs on my computer
- Stressful
- It sucks
- Boring
- Pointless
- Citing sources
- Analyzing sources
- Failure imminent
- Where do I start?
- Create new knowledge
- I don't want to do it

The class then transitions from this brainstorming activity to a series of questions Heidi asks them, such as, "How did you decide which teams to choose for the NCAA March Madness Bracket?" "How did you decide to attend this college?" "What's in style for fall?" "What will the weather be like this weekend?" The class is then directed to a discussion of how they would locate the information necessary to answer any of those questions and what types of sources would be appropriate for the different kinds of information being sought.

Larson (1982) points out that research can take many different forms and that it is used for different purposes. The brainstorming/questions illustrates to the students that they are performing research all the time, and it rarely culminates in a formal research essay. The purpose of the research is to use the best source to gain information for use in a variety of ways.

Because one of the fundamental core objectives for most first-year composition courses is to teach research skills, instructors must focus more heavily on teaching research skills as an activity. Simply teaching a formal research-based essay inadvertently teaches students that if "there is a kind of writing that incorporates the results of research, there are (by implication) many kinds of writing that do not and need not do so" (Larson, 1982, p. 814). The students then perceive research as something only necessary for a formal research-based essay.

Larson (1982) maintains that teaching research as an *activity* serves as "a reminder that responsible writing normally depends on well-planned investigation of data" (p. 814). To teach research effectively then, students must learn to approach research as an activity that may or may not be used formally.

When Heidi first asks her students about their attitudes about writing, they are generally resistant, hesitant, and even afraid of the process. Yet once she establishes that they do research all the time for a variety of daily inquiries, their attitudes begin to shift to viewing research as a transferable skill, and more importantly, a skill they're already using all the time.

GETTING STUDENTS INVESTED IN THEIR RESEARCH

In "'This is Cool!' Multigenre Research Reports," Timothy Cate (2000) writes that students have been taught for too long that "formal thesis research papers and oral presentations of research findings were the only options for the students" (p. 127). Sirpa Grierson (1999) writes that it is important to find ways to encourage deeper engagement with the research. Seeing research as something done for more than a formal essay allows students to more deeply engage in intellectual creativity.

Tom Romano's *Writing With Passion* highlights the importance for "creativity and imagination [to] be part of research" (Romano, 1995, p. 130). Dickson et al. (2002) conclude that our traditional ways of teaching research to students stifles "creativity and lacks personal investment" (p. 83). All of these findings support the experiences experiences Heidi and Michael have found in their classrooms over the last decade. Students dread research, they use it to find facts to support things they already know, they don't know how to find strong sources, their final projects lack a student voice, and they see little value in learning to write a formal research paper.

Over the course of many semesters, it has become clear that college writing instructors need to approach the researching component of the first-year composition classroom differently. The goal isn't to eliminate the research-based essay (it's still a critical component of the first-year composition course) but instead to teach research skills better so that the research-based outcome, whether it be a chart or an essay, more effectively communicates the findings of the writer.

THE RESEARCH PROJECT

So how did the authors get to the research project as a viable alternative to the formal research-based paper? The idea emerged one afternoon after class as they lamented how tedious it was to teach the traditional research-based essay. The students weren't engaged, and the research was subpar at best. Michael mentioned trying something similar to Tom Romano's project in *Blending Genre, Altering Style: Writing Multigenre Papers*.

Romano describes the multigenre research project as a series of "crots" or individual pieces of writing that come together to create a new text. These crots are of varying length and represent a variety of genres, but they work together to create one unified project (Romano, 2000). Grierson (1999) claims that the multigenre project allows us to "'meld fact, interpretation, and imagination' into a series of self-contained pieces" (p. 51).

Romano has written extensively of how to successfully integrate a multigenre research project in middle school and high school English classrooms, but could the same principles be applied to the writing and research skills necessary in a college composition course? To evaluate this, Heidi and Michael reviewed the course objective for ENG 101 at their current institution. The objectives are as follows:

Students will:

- Encounter opportunities to write for different rhetorical situations
- Learn strategies for different rhetorical situations
- Have the ability to analyze and produce texts guided by basic rhetorical decisions
- Practice critical reading skills, including the ability to identify genre conventions and evaluate claims and evidence
- Demonstrate effective research process, including gathering academic and non-academic sources, and assessing sources for quality and suitability to purpose
- Synthesize source material and integrate into your own writing to support a clearly defined thesis
- Employ syntax appropriate to different rhetorical situations.

These basic core course objectives are reflective of and supported by both the National Council of Teachers of English and the Council of Writing Program Administrators. (For a comprehensive overview of the learning outcomes, please visit these two professional organization's websites.)

It is clear that the overall expectation of college writing courses is for students to learn *transferable* writing skills to a variety of rhetorical situations and genres and not simply to create one conventional research-based essay for assessment in a first-year writing course. In theory, a multigenre research project would meet these objectives not only sufficiently but far better than a conventional research-based essay could.

You can see from table 1.1 that the multigenre research project meets and even exceeds the criteria established for core outcomes for the college writing course.

Published research indicates that the multigenre research project encourages more intentional choices for different rhetorical situations (Davis & Shadle, 2007). It allows the student voice to emerge in ways that traditional research essays prohibit (Davis & Shadle, 2007). The multigenre research project encourages deeper engagement with the research and teaches research as a process, not a product (Paré, Starke-Meyerring, & McAlpine, 2006).

The multigenre research project helps the students see the transferability of their research skills to other genres and rhetorical situations (Cate, 2000). It teaches different ways to integrate and cite source material. Critical thinking skills are enhanced as the students find connections between academia and life outside the ivory tower (Dickson et al. 2002). The multigenre research project broadens the student's understanding of a controlling idea and allows for creativity without compromising core learning outcomes of a basic writing course (LeNoir, 2002).

Table 1.1 A Comparison of Core Objectives and Learning Outcomes

First-Year Composition Core Objectives	Learning Outcomes of a Multigenre Research Project
• Opportunities to write for different rhetorical situations • Strategies for different rhetorical situations • Ability to analyze and produce texts guided by basic rhetorical decisions • Practice critical reading skills, including the ability to identify genre conventions, evaluate claims and evidence • Demonstrate effective research process, including gathering academic and non-academic sources and assessing sources for quality and suitability to purpose • Synthesize source material and integrate into your own writing to support a clearly defined thesis • Employ syntax appropriate to different rhetorical situations	• Deeper engagement with the research • Teaches research as a process, not a product • Demands more intentional rhetorical choices • Shows transferability of research skills to other forms of writing • Teaches different ways to integrate and cite source material • Allows the student voice to emerge in writing • Critical thinking skills enhanced • Teaches more genres • Allows for creativity without compromising core learning outcomes of a basic writing course • Allows students to find connections between academia and beyond • Broadens concept of controlling idea

The rationale for using a multigenre research project in the first-year composition course.

Justification of the MGRP in the Freshman Composition Classroom 9

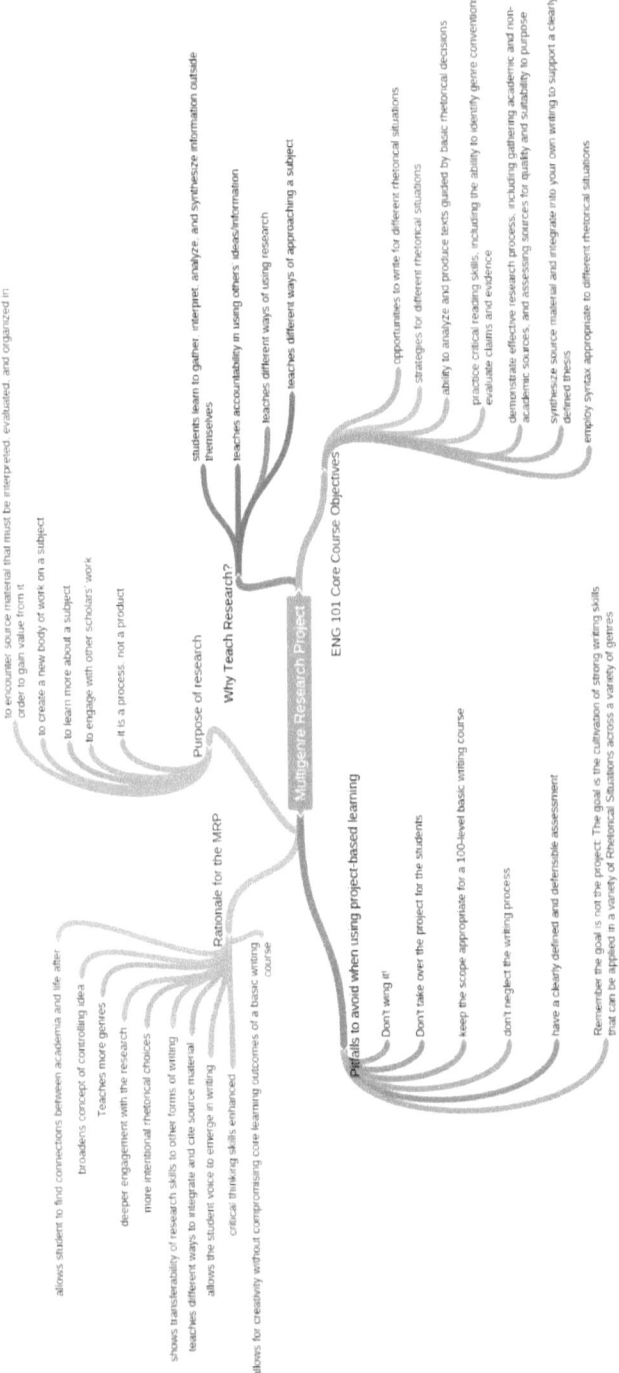

Figure 1.1 Why the Multigenre Research Project Works

If done carefully and intentionally, in theory, the multigenre research project would satisfy the goals of the first-year composition course far better than a traditional research-based paper could by providing a better understanding of what research is and how it is used, encouraging a variety of genres for presenting the research, and encouraging students to be mindful of the specific rhetorical choices that would need to be made in order to complete a unified project.

Of course, theory doesn't always translate to actual success in the classroom. To that end, Heidi and Michael set out to provide conclusive evidence that the multigenre research project that Romano used successfully in middle school and high school classrooms could indeed be adapted for successful integration into the college classroom.

In the spring semester of 2014, the authors conducted a semester-long study of three classes of first-year composition students. The student demographic was forty-seven freshmen, twenty sophomores, six juniors, and two seniors. Prior to the multigenre research project, the students were polled on their attitudes toward research and writing research papers. This small sampling of responses is indicative of the overall attitude across all three sections.

- *"When someone says 'research paper' I dread what comes next."* Carl, senior
- *"When I hear 'research' I think of looking up information online."* Emily, freshman
- *"When I think of research papers, I associate them with having boring topics. These are typically of little to no interest to me."* Claire, freshman
- *"The first thing I think of is how much writing one sucks."* Ryan, sophomore
- *"I see countless amounts of hours researching."* Jessica, sophomore
- *"When I think of a research paper, I think of a long, boring paper based on something I'm not interested in but am required to write about."* Mariah, freshman
- *"Research papers are intimidating to me."* Chris, freshman

This list could include seventy-five similar student responses reflecting an attitude of a sense of dread, tedium, and uselessness when it comes to research. However, by the end of the project, their attitudes toward research are markedly different. The students were asked the question, "What has been most surprising for you in the process of researching and creating the multigenre research project?"

The student responses reflect a conclusive attitude shift about research.

- *"I'm surprised how fun this project actually is. It is fun to be able to be creative while also providing credible information from scholarly sources."* Jacob, freshman

- *"All the different kinds of sources!" Ben, sophomore*
- *"The various scholarly places that I was able to find information about my topic. Before this unit, I had no idea I was so bad at researching." Elizabeth, sophomore*
- *"The most exciting part of this whole process so far has defiantly [sic] been the research process. I'm usually not the one who likes to research, but the fact that these are the topics we were able to pick and I picked such an interesting one just makes it so much more enjoyable." Cael, freshman*
- *"The most surprising to me is how fun and exciting this type of project makes research become. I use to hate having to do research papers . . . [this] has made it surprisingly enjoyable to want to do research." Trevor, freshman*

The study asked the students at the conclusion of the semester to evaluate their experiences in creating a multigenre research project for ENG 101. Using a 1–5 Likert scale, the students responded to a series of questions. The findings (see table 1.2) were exactly what the study hoped to show.

The research study also offered space for students to respond to ten short-answer questions (see Appendix A for complete list of questions and answers). One of the questions posed to the students was, "What did you learn about writing in different genres for different rhetorical situations?" Anonymous student responses include:

- *You must know your reader*
- *You need to make different rhetorical choices when writing in different genres*
- *There are more genres than I thought and we use them in our daily lives*
- *Target Audience!*
- *Certain information is better suited for certain situations*
- *Writing with researched content takes many forms*

The other telling question was, "Would you recommend this project for future use? Why or why not?" The responses to this question are overwhelmingly positive (responses were anonymous):

- *YES! It was very enjoyable and I felt it worth taking my freshman year*
- *Yes. It is far more applicable than an 11-page traditional research paper*
- *Yes. It does what a research paper can't do: interest a student*
- *Yes. It made my writing stronger*
- *Yes. It allows students to use their creativity*

Overall, the anonymous student responses reflect an attitude of satisfaction with the project. Most students said that the project was fun, allowed

Table 1.2 Student Responses for End of Semester Survey

Question	Range	Median	Number Responding
1. I enjoyed the Multigenre Research Project (MGRP)	2–5	4.4	53
2. I have gained strong research skills from writing the MGRP.	3–5	4.6	53
3. I can locate quality research more effectively than I could prior to completing the MGRP for ENG 101.	3–5	4.6	53
4. I can evaluate source material more effectively than I could prior to completing the MGRP for ENG 101.	3–5	4.5	53
5. I can read, understand, and summarize source material more effectively than I could prior to completing the MGRP for ENG 101.	2–5	4.4	53
6. I have learned a variety of methods for using and citing source material as a result of my work with the MGRP in ENG 101.	3–5	4.6	52
7. I can use formal documentation style when appropriate (specifically APA).	3–5	4.7	52
8. My writing skills were challenged and polished through writing the MGRP.	3–5	4.4	52
9. The MGRP took an appropriate amount of time relevant to a 100-level basic writing course.	1–5	4.2	52
10. I understood how the MGRP was going to be assessed by my instructor.	2–5	4.5	52
11. I believe that the rubric provided by my instructor offered a fair assessment for the work I submitted.	3–5	4.5	52
12. A MGRP prepared me for writing in "the real world" as well as or better than a traditional researched academic paper might have.	3–5	4.5	52
13. I understand how research is a process as much as it is an outcome.	3–5	4.5	52
14. I used the writing process (brainstorming, prewriting, drafting, revising, editing, proofing) in the creation of my MGRP.	2–5	4.4	52

Student responses to the "Effectiveness of a Multigenre Research Project in the Basic Writing Course Student Survey" administered in Spring 2015.

for creativity for the students, and deepened their understanding of how to approach research.

Not only did the integration of the multigenre research project meet the students' expectations of the quality of learning from the unit, their final projects far exceeded the course expectations for the unit. The depth of research, careful use of appropriate sources, and thoughtfulness of the final projects are markedly more impressive than any student work that Heidi or Michael had previously encountered.

The project allowed the students to find and use their voices in their writing. Every project was incredibility unique and reflected the interests and values of the writer. The final projects had strong unity (with a clearly defined controlling idea), represented a wide variety of genres and rhetorical choices and indicated a depth of research as an activity that went well beyond "jumping on the internet to find some stuff." Most importantly, the final projects clearly illustrated that the students had mastered the core course objectives for ENG 101.

Heidi and Michael's research study provides the quantitative evidence needed to support the effectiveness of using a multigenre research project in the college classroom. Formal assessment of the final projects and the students' self-assessment of the skills learned show strong mastery of the course's core objectives having been met. The study showed that the multigenre research project could move from theory to practice through a successful integration into the college writing course.

However, the quantitative evidence only shows a small piece of the successful integration of this project. This was, by far and away, the most engaged semester of students Heidi had ever taught. Not only were the students doing better research, they were actually *enjoying* their research. They were engaged in their projects in a way that she had not seen before. In fact, Heidi was so impressed that she had a colleague come to observe her classroom so she could show her what the students were working on.

As the visiting teacher walked around the room, the students readily explained their individual projects to her and then said, "You should go see X's project, too! It's really cool!" The students were showing engagement in the research of the *other* students in the class! Later that week, Heidi met with her colleague to review the colleague's observation of the class. Her colleague was clearly blown away by what she had observed. Her excitement for the potential of this type of writing project reinforces Heidi and Michael's belief in the impact this type of project can have on all first-year writing courses at the college level.

INTEGRATING A MULTIGENRE RESEARCH PROJECT INTO YOUR SYLLABUS

This first chapter simply provides the justification and evidence for the effectiveness of using a multigenre research project in a college classroom for the first-year writing courses based on a research study performed by Heidi and Michael in spring 2015. The study provides clear evidence of the successful integration of a multigenre research project in three first-year-composition courses as a stand-alone unit within the syllabus.

Now to get to the fun part.

Exactly how does one go about integrating this into the syllabus? In the next chapter, Heidi will detail how she structured the entire semester to include a stand-alone unit for the multigenre research project. Then, in the following chapter, Michael will illustrate how this type of project can be implemented as a semester-long project. Finally, the authors will provide ideas for assessment and some specific examples of student work.

REFERENCES

Bazerman, C. (2007). Genres and cognitive development: Beyond writing to learn. In C. Bazerman, A. Bonini, & D. Figueiredo (Eds.), *Genre in a changing world* (pp. 279–294). West Lafayette, IN: WAC Clearinghouse Parlor Press. Retrieved from http://wac.colostate.edu/books/genre/.

Cate, T. (2000). "This is cool!" Multigenre research reports. *The Social Studies, 91*(3), 137–140. doi: 10.1080/00377990009602457.

Davis, R., & Shadle, M. (2000, February). "Building a Mystery": Alternative research writing and the academic act of seeking. *College Composition and Communication, 51*(3), 417–446.

Davis, R., & Shadle, M. (2007). *Teaching multiwriting: Researching and composing with multiple genres, media, disciplines, and cultures.* Carbondale, IL: Southern Illinois University Press.

Dickson, R., DeGraff, J., & Foard, M. (2002). Learning about self and others through multigenre research projects. *The English Journal, 92*(2), 82-90. doi: 10.2307/822230.

Grierson, S. (1999). Circling through text: Teaching research through multigenre writing. *The English Journal, 89*(1), 51–55. doi: 10.2307/821356.

Kolowich, S. (2011). What students don't know. *Inside Higher Ed.* Retrieved from https://www.insidehighered.com.

Larson, R. (1982). The "Research Paper" in the writing course: A non-form of writing. *College English, 44*(8), 811–816. doi: 10.2307/822230.

LeNoir, W. D. (2002). The multigenre warning label. *The English Journal, 92*(2), 99–101. doi: 10.2307/822232.

Paré, A., Starke-Meyerring, D., & McAlpine, L. (2006). The dissertation as: Many readers, many readings. In C. Bazerman, A. Bonini, & D. Figueiredo (Eds.), *Genre in a changing world* (pp. 179–193). West Lafayette, IN: WAC Clearinghouse Parlor Press. Retrieved from http://wac.colostate.edu/books/genre/chapter9.pdf.

Pirie, B. (1997). *Reshaping high school English.* United States: National Council of Teachers of English.

Romano, T. (1995). *Writing with Passion: Life Stories, Multiple Genres.* Portsmouth, NH: Boynton & Cook.

Romano, T. (2000). *Blending genre, altering style.* Portsmouth, NH: Heinemann.

Chapter 2

The Self-Contained Unit for the MGRP

INTRODUCTION TO THE SELF-CONTAINED UNIT FOR THE MGRP

The multigenre research project (MGRP) can be taught as a stand-alone semester-long class or it can be taught as a contained unit embedded within the syllabus. Whichever method you choose, there are some practical things to keep in mind as you approach the MGRP. In this chapter, Heidi demonstrates the scaffolding in learning she uses to prepare the students for success in the MGRP as a stand-alone unit. She then provides the outline of a unit to use over a six-week time frame.

The students' success with the stand-alone unit for the MGRP is highly dependent on their familiarity in four specific areas:

1. Thesis statements and how they create the purpose and unity in pieces of writing
2. Rhetorical situation, specifically audience and form
3. Proper integration of secondary source material
4. Students' ability to access and assess credible and appropriate research

Heidi typically spends the first two weeks of a new semester focusing heavily on thesis statements and the rhetorical situation. She often starts the discussion by asking her students to imagine they are stranded in the middle of an ocean. Would they start paddling furiously and hope to eventually find the shore? Would they wait until dark and try to read the stars? What would their plan be? Would they start with a plan or only settle on a plan after futilely trying to navigate without one? This metaphor helps direct students into the discussion of writing with purpose: If you just start writing with no purpose or guiding plan in place, it's kind of like paddling furiously and hoping that happenstance will lead you to shore, or in the case for students, a decent piece of writing will emerge.

In a traditional piece of writing, the thesis statement defines the purpose of the writing, which directs the research process, the outlining process, and the completion of the draft. What makes the MGRP more challenging than a traditional essay is that students are expected to create numerous pieces of writing in several different genres that are all leading purposefully to one unified theme for the project. If there is no clear purpose at the outset, the project often falls apart from lack of unity and simply becomes a compilation of various artifacts.

Students are unable to accomplish this in the MGRP if they don't already have a firm understanding of what the role of a thesis statement is, how to write a strong thesis statement, and how to use it to direct their research and content. For this reason, the first two units of the semester should focus heavily on the structure and purpose of the thesis statement to develop the main points. Once the students have a clear understanding of purpose and unity, these skills can then be applied in unit three to the MGRP.

Additionally, students must have a basic understanding of what the rhetorical situation is. In *Rhetoric*, Aristotle defined rhetoric as the "faculty of observing in any given case the available means of persuasion." He maintained that the *rhetor* must keep the subject, the audience, and the speaker in mind when determining how to approach a speaking situation. In a first-year composition class, this translates into purpose, audience, stance, genre, and design, and is often taught in conjunction with Aristotle's *logos, ethos*, and *pathos*.

For first-year composition students, the rhetorical situation feels like something new and difficult. Heidi first tries to break that misconception down by demonstrating to students that they are making rhetorical choices every day, particularly in the area of audience awareness. She then applies it to writing and teaches students that awareness of the rhetorical situation should directly impact every piece of writing they ever produce.

Heidi emphasizes to students that writing is only successful if it effectively communicates with the intended audience. To ensure that students have a firm grasp of this piece of the rhetorical situation, audience awareness is the second major focus of the first two weeks of the course. To help make the rhetorical situation more accessible to students, Heidi talks specifically about audience expectations using "real-life examples" as much as possible.

One way to open up the discussion on audience awareness is to ask the students the difference between getting dressed for an interview at McDonalds versus dressing for an interview in the human resources office of the college. What are the audiences' expectations in each situation? What happens when the interviewee doesn't meet the expectations?

Heidi continues to focus on audience awareness through units 1 and 2. She reminds students that they are writing for a perceived academic audience not just for the instructor. She helps them understand why writing to a specific audience is critical to their success in communicating through writing, whether it's a cover letter, a scholarship application, or a traditional paper for another class. This groundwork helps establish the framework for understanding audience expectations within different genres and then applying this knowledge to the MGRP.

The third most important framework that must be in place for students to succeed in the MGRP is the integration of secondary sources using a formal documentation style. Heidi teaches APA documentation style because very few of her students are humanities majors, but it doesn't matter which documentation style the instructor chooses. What matters is that the students understand how to locate credible source material and then integrate the source material into their writing. This is, after all, one of the basic learning objectives of most first-year college writing courses.

Heidi teaches source integration through a scaffolding process throughout the entire semester. First she uses a response essay and then an informative essay to establish the groundwork for the MGRP. There are many different essay types that would work well for this groundwork, so don't feel limited to what Heidi has used. Ultimately, the goal is to bring students to a competency in the aforementioned skills: purposeful writing, awareness of the rhetorical situation, assessment of source credibility/appropriateness, and formal source integration.

In the first unit, Heidi's students write a response essay that requires the integration of four direct quotes from two predetermined articles. The students are assessed on content and structure as well as their abilities to (1) integrate direct quotes correctly and (2) create a proper references page. Students are required to use APA documentation for their quotations, but they are not assessed on their mastery of it.

In the second unit, the students write a research-based informative essay. In this essay, the students are required to integrate source material from four secondary sources to develop their content. The supporting material must be tightly related to the thesis statement and be integrated through a balanced use of direct quotations and summaries or paraphrases. The use of proper APA style documentation is required as well as a formal references page. Heidi spends a fair amount of time during this unit teaching the students how to properly synthesize sources and cite source material. This is a great time to discuss why writers credit their sources.

Using credible research is imperative for student writers, but few students have the research skills necessary to succeed in an academic setting. Both of these first two units encourage students to begin building off the research of other experts to support their own thesis statements. In the first unit, students are given the specific sources to respond to and asked only to provide direct quotes (the simplest way to integrate source material).

In the second unit, the research requirement is expanded and now the student must show a deeper understanding of using source material by including summary and paraphrases. This unit also focuses on the synthesizing of numerous sources for content development. Many students find this to be especially challenging as they are accustomed to using one source per main point instead of using multiple sources for each main point.

Locating credible and appropriate sources is also a conundrum for many students. Too often the student's first impulse is to use a general search engine. Therefore, it is a valuable use of time to teach the students how to use the internet for research. Because sources are supplied in the first unit, Heidi uses the second unit to teach students ways to critically assess websites for credibility. A fair amount of time is spent teaching students the vital difference between "trolling the web" and using the web for research.

Heidi then begins to shift the students away from general web searches and into the library databases. Most students have never encountered an academic search of this nature, and it is a frustrating process for them. General search engines allow vague keyword searches. Databases for academic journals do not. Heidi has devised several online search activities to facilitate the exploration of online databases for students (examples are included in chapter 4). At this point in the semester, Heidi's goal is make students aware of the various tools available for locating research and to teach them how to use this research to develop the content of their own writing.

Once the students have a strong understanding of purposeful writing through a strong controlling idea, awareness of the rhetorical situation, familiarity with a formal documentation style, and the ability to locate strong supporting sources, they are ready to be introduced to the MGRP. This is where the fun really starts. As Heidi says in class, "Let the adventure begin."

UNVEILING THE PROJECT

The authors have already established that the purpose of the MGRP is to teach stronger research skills and engagement with source material. For the self-contained unit, the MGRP is assigned after completing a response essay and a research-based informative essay. The students have studied APA and should have some mastery of it by now. They are acquainted with library research in terms of locating and using sources. And yet, at this point in the semester, it's very typical for students to still view research as an onerous task with only one outcome: a formally assessed essay. It's good to remember this as you begin the MGRP unit.

Heidi teaches the MGRP unit over six weeks (twelve class periods). This is to accommodate substantial in-class work time for the students. There are many practical reasons for including these work days in the class calendar, but the most valuable reason is simple: Students have direct access to the instructor *while* they are performing their research and writing their various genres. Students are able to engage in conversations about their projects *during* the process of writing.

Heidi has found this to be immeasurably valuable in teaching students. Instead of saying, "Go back and fix this" she can say, "Let's try this here instead." By extension, students spend much less time redoing their work. They are able to ask for guidance and immediately apply the feedback. The other logical reason for having in-class work time included in the calendar is that it alleviates some of the stress of time management for the students. Knowing they'll have time to work in class helps their focus remain on the writing and not the deadline.

When the MGRP is first introduced, the students will likely be overwhelmed and afraid but cautiously intrigued. This is natural because the assignment appears on the surface to be monstrous in scope, and it deviates from the traditional assignments they've encountered in their academic careers. At the beginning of the introduction of the unit, go ahead and assure your students that it's okay to be confused and that they'll be feeling a lot more comfortable with the assignment by the end of the class period.

Day 1: How to Pitch the Project and Get Student Buy-In

Objective:

- To explore attitudes about research and introduce the MGRP unit
- To introduce the MGRP writing assignment (a formal assignment sheet is included in the appendix)

First, assign a reading assignment that discusses the indefensibility of the research essay as a stand-alone assignment such as "The 'Research Paper' in the Writing Course: A Non-Form of Writing" by Richard Larson.[1] At the beginning of class, have a five minute conversation on the content of the essay and then quickly transition to a free writing assignment. For ten minutes, have the students respond to the questions "What does a research essay mean for you?" and "What do you expect to learn from doing a research-based essay?"

After students have had time to organize their thoughts in the free write, have them share and write the responses on the board. In Heidi's experience, the lists typically include all the responses you would expect, from "gathering information" to it being "a colossal waste of time." Once students realize it is okay to say "research sucks!" the authenticity of their responses increases dramatically. As expected, their responses typically reflect an attitude that research is boring and not applicable outside of the college composition classroom.

Now that the class has established that research is pointless and meaningless to them, it's time to turn them on their heads. Heidi does this by asking a variety of questions: How did you know how to fill out your March Madness Brackets or how to choose your players for the NFL Fantasy Football Draft? How did you decide to come to this university? How do you know what's in fashion for the next season? How do you decide what to include in a scholarship application, cover letter, or resume?

The purpose in asking these questions is to highlight that students perform research all the time and it rarely culminates in a formal research paper. Doing this begins to deconstruct the attitude that research is an activity with only an academic outcome. The other important thing these questions do is allow Heidi to show the students how the "expert" sources will vary depending on the topic choice and the intended presentation of the findings. It also allows her to show how there are different genres for different purposes of research, such as using a March Madness Bracket versus a formal study on college athletes.

The students are then asked to create a list of the skills they have already practiced this semester that will help them be successful in a project like the MGRP. As the class discusses the list, Heidi reinforces how the previous two essays have prepared them to be successful in scholarly research as well as "real-world writing scenarios," because the skills they've practiced are transferable: purpose, controlling idea (thesis), sound research skills, integration of research, and overall unity in the project.

At this point, some are a little freaked out because they can't fathom how one thesis statement will cover the scope of the project. To mitigate this a little, Heidi displays a list of a hundred topics (or so) and randomly chooses a few. (A general list of topics is available in the appendix.) For each one, she narrows the subject to a manageable topic and creates a working thesis statement for the class. For example, take the topic of wrestling and narrow it down. Wrestling, Olympic wrestling, Dave Schultz (American Olympian), violence in wrestling. From this brainstorming, the topic becomes: Dave Schultz, an American Olympic wrestler who was shot and killed by his coach.

Next she shows the class real student examples of the MGRP.[2] In this case, she starts with the student's project that actually was about Dave Schultz. After three or so examples, the students begin to be more comfortable with the MGRP, see the numerous possibilities available to them, and become excited about choosing their own topics for research.

At the end of the first day of the MGRP Unit, Heidi has the students do a ten-minute self-reflective piece of writing responding to the question "What concerns do you have the MGRP? What interests you about the project?" This accomplishes two important purposes: (1) It allows the instructor to understand what the main concerns for the student are (or what pieces of the assignment introduction weren't clear) and (2) It allows the student to have time to consider what the project might mean for them personally. Inevitably, a sense of excitement emerges as students realize they're in control of their topics as well as the overall scope of their projects.

The study the authors performed elicited these responses from students:

- *"I am somewhat excited to start the Multigenre Research Project. My uncertainty is due to the amount of content."* Ethan, sophomore, project focus: Lean Manufacturing
- *"I feel this project will be fun to write."* Jeremy, sophomore, project focus: Spartacus
- *"I am confident in my ability to research this topic, and excited to write a project like this because it is a new type of paper for me."* Kathryn, sophomore, project focus: Woodstock
- *"I usually think of research projects as boring and hard work, but I think this project will be interesting because I was able to choose my topic. It will be fun to learn more about my favorite athlete."* Emily, junior, project focus: Joe Mauer
- *"I think that the Multigenre Research Project will be a good learning experience."* Cassidy, sophomore, project focus: Applying to Veterinarian School

This reflective writing also reveals, time and again, a prevalent concern about the "creativity" component of the project. Many students include "I hate being creative" or "I don't have a creative bone in my body" in this free write. You can help ease this concern by talking about student voice in writing—meaning the overall project will exude some tone: funny, entertaining, serious, dark, sad, etc. The creativity component doesn't have to be a song or a poem or a drawing. It could simply be how all the research is assembled to create an interesting project about the chosen topic.

Day 2: Investigating Genre

Objective:

- That every student leaves today with a solid understanding of what a genre is and how it applies to literature, movies, art, writing, and more

specifically, the MGRP. This will be accomplished through a student-directed genre activity.³
- Review student topic submissions.⁴

One of the core learning objectives for most college composition classrooms is the ability to write across different genres. Many students come to the classroom with little or no idea of what a genre actually is. Because students have to have a concrete understanding of what a genre is to be successful in the MGRP, Heidi assigns a couple of articles on genre for students to read prior to class and then devotes the first part of the class period to a mini-lecture on genre to reinforce the readings.⁵

The goal for this class period is to help the students better understand (1) what genre is and (2) why it's important to understand the conventions of the genres they choose to use. The MGRP requires students to use several different genres in their final projects. Heidi requires a minimum of five different genres in the final project, only two of which are predetermined: a summary/background informative essay and an annotated bibliography; beyond that, the students are allowed to choose which genres work best with their topics.

To help students understand genre, Heidi asks students to think about movies. She gives the illustration of how sometimes we go to watch a movie in a specific genre and are disappointed when the movie fails to meet the expectations of the genre. For example, if you choose a comedy, you expect it to be funny. If it ends up being a serious movie, you're disappointed. Knowing the type of genre prepares the audience for what to expect. In the same way, when writing, genres give the reader an expectation of what the writing's purpose is. When it fails to meet expectation, the reader is confused.

Additionally, it's important to determine the rhetorical situation prior to choosing the genre. For example, if you are announcing the death of a person, there are several genres available to do so: obituary, epitaph, email, text, memorial service bulletin, etc. Knowing which method your receiver expects to receive that news through will determine which genre you choose to communicate that message. Likewise, a resume for a business position at IBM will look dramatically different than a curriculum vitae for an academic teaching position.

These simple illustrations help the students begin making the connection between genre and audience awareness. Teaching students to write for different rhetorical situations is not only important for transferable writing skills across disciplines, it's also a valuable life skill across diverse professions.

After reviewing the concept of genre, it's useful to provide an activity that reinforces the concept. To this means, Heidi created an activity that requires students to investigate an assigned genre and then create a research-based piece of writing within the conventions of their assigned genres.⁶ This activity provides the students with a stronger understanding of genre, it reinforces audience awareness, and it illustrates how unity works (and doesn't work) across genres contained in one project.

On a very practical point, at the start of class, the students should turn in their topic proposals. Try to assess and comment on the submissions while the students work on the genre activity. The feedback on this is vital to the students' successfully choosing strong topics. The topics will be as diverse as the students.

Heidi really encourages them to choose topics on subjects they don't already know a lot about or something they really want to learn more about. Heidi extends some grace in the submission of the proposal because it's vital that every student turn it in for feedback. If it's possible to provide both written and oral feedback at this time, the students will be well prepared to begin their projects.

Day 3: The Writing Process for Success in the MGRP

Objective:

- By the end of today's class period, students should feel comfortable with the MGRP assignment.
- Students should have a strong start on the research for their individual topics.
- Students should have a minimum of an outline complete for Assignment #1: Summary/Background Information.[7]

By Day 3, the students are beginning to become interested in how their projects will turn out and they're starting to worry about the looming submission date of Assignment #1: Summary/Background. They don't have a clear vision for their projects yet, but they are working to find one. Heidi finds that this a good day to devote a large amount of class time to self-directed research.

If you review Heidi's assignment sheet for the MGRP, you will see that she has made two genres of the final project required: (1) Summary/Background informative essay and (2) annotated bibliography. The rationale for this is twofold. One, students need a grounding piece for their projects. They need a piece that can provide the overview and establish the context for the information that will follow. Heidi also requires that this piece adhere to formal APA documentation style. This reinforces one of the course's core objectives of mastery in use of formal documentation of research.

The annotated bibliography also meets a course objective for ethical use of source material. It helps students (1) organize their research and (2) evaluate the sources they are encountering. Because this isn't due until later in the unit, a full discussion of the annotated bibliography will follow later in this chapter.

Heidi likes to start Day 3 of the MGRP unit with an in-class free write activity based on the two articles: "Circling through the Text: Teaching Research through Multigenre Writing" by Sirpa Grierson and "'This is Cool!' Multigenre Research Reports" by Timothy Cate. The students should come to class having already read the two articles, so they can begin a response writing immediately.

After the free write, go ahead and have a class discussion about what the scope of the project looks like. It's also a great time to pull up some student samples again to reinforce (and sometimes recalibrate) what the final project will look like. It's a nice opportunity for students to share their concerns and worries with their peers. They often find that their concerns are normal, which gives them a boost in confidence for the project.

After the discussion, break the class into smaller groups to discuss their specific projects. This allows the students to verbally express some of the ideas that have been floating around in their heads. It also allows them to get a sense of where the content might need to be directed to sustain the reader's attention. It's fine to give them a fair amount of time to discuss their projects. As the instructor, you can float around to the various groups and help direct their conversations as necessary.

Eventually, Heidi brings the group discussions to a close to redirect the class discussion toward content and what depth of content is expected in a college-level project of this nature. She also addresses the requirement of creativity. The students often have a difficult time understanding what academic creativity means. The first things they think of are poems, songs, creative fiction, or art.

Heidi challenges students to think more deeply about the concept of creativity by asking the question: What's the difference between a story that is made up and a narrative that is based on research? In "Learning About Self and Others Through Multigenre Research Projects," Dickson et al. (2002) state that the exercise of "making interpretations of the sources [students] were reading" is an important skill for students to make meaning of texts (p. 85).

Intellectual creativity can be about filling in the gaps based on facts, much like historians do (Dickson et al., 2002). In *Blending Genre, Altering Style: Writing Multigenre Papers*, Romano (2000) maintains that a MGRP allows writers to "combine fact with imagination . . . to render scenes that actually happened but whose details have been lost" (p. 68). This is one of the major differences between a traditional-based research paper and a MGRP. The room for creativity is immense, if based on sound research.

Intellectual creativity involves finding connections and links where others have overlooked them. It's drawing viable conclusions from inconclusive research. It's creating new and interesting ways to think about old, mundane things. It's taking a worn, tired topic and finding a new way to present the information to excite a new audience.

Additionally, Heidi gives the students a wide berth for creativity in their projects. She allows the students to hypothesize the moments between the facts that are published based on the question "what is plausible based on what you've encountered in the research?" This really helps students understand the difference between creative writing and research-based "fiction based on fact" (Dickson et al., 2002, p. 85).

To illustrate, Heidi provides a couple of examples of how fiction based on fact could play a role in the MGRP. Take the topic of the Battle of the Bulge. A student could include a personal letter from a soldier to his lover written on Christmas Day. From the student's research, the student would know that it was cold and there was a cease-fire that day. The Germans and Americans played cards. They celebrated the holiday and then went back to their foxholes that night and continued the war in the morning. The fictional letter, based on facts, could address the relief of the cease-fire, the incessant cold, and the desire to be home on American soil.

As the students begin to process a new definition of creativity, they will become noticeably more relaxed with the requirement. In fact, they often become a little more excited about the creative component as they consider the new and interesting genres they had previously overlooked as "not applicable to my topic."

The rest of the class period is time well spent if you can allow the students to work independently on their projects. The students really value this time because it allows the instructor to walk around the classroom and touch base with students one-on-one as they delve into their various topics. Heidi often helps them reframe their search terms to find new, unexplored areas for usable source material. The students appreciate the extra in-class work time, and they benefit hugely because they have access to immediate feedback on their process.

Day 4: Peer Review and Workshop of Assignment #1

Objective:

- Students should come to class with a complete draft of Assignment #1.
- The focus of class will be on peer review and revision of this first piece in their MGRP, which will be turned in for assessment at the end of the class period.

The success of the entire project depends on the strength of this first piece of writing, so it needs to be well done. Unfortunately, for a variety of reasons, students will show up with a lackluster submission for the background/summary piece. It is generally because students ignored the prewriting, their topic isn't focused enough, their research is incomplete, or they just haven't really put forth the effort to revise the piece yet. Do not despair. It's very normal. The MGRP is still new to them, and students are just beginning to understand the scope of research and depth of content that the project will require.

Have the students bring two copies of Assignment #1 to class—one is for submission (for a quick review by the instructor) and the other is for peer review. This allows for two things to happen during this class period: (1) The instructor can quickly review the turned in drafts for any glaring issues and return them at the end of the class period and (2) the students can use a peer workshop to both give and receive feedback on this first piece of the project.

Before dividing the students into peer groups for workshop, have every student highlight their thesis statement in Assignment #1. If one is not identifiable, encourage them to return to the original proposal and determine what the purpose for the project is. After this is completed, have the students exchange essays and begin the self-directed workshop.[8] Heidi has noted that as students begin to share their projects with each other, the energy in the room heightens. Most of the students, by this point, are becoming genuinely interested in their projects.

While the students are workshopping their essays, quickly review the drafts and then conference briefly with students individually to discuss any major issues. It tends to be the case that the students have a lot of questions. Meeting with each student individually is also helpful in alleviating their concerns and keeping them on track.

At the end of the class period, let the students know that they will each need to bring a folder to the next class period. This "Process Folder" will need to contain all the brainstorming, drafts, research notes, etc. that are used in the creation of the final submission of the formal MGRP. It is essentially the "proof" of their writing process. Let students know you will collect these periodically for three reasons: (1) to hold the students accountable for meeting the benchmarks of the project, (2) to catch any glaring issues before the final submission, and (3) to eliminate the temptation to plagiarize the project.

You can decide if you want to formally assess Assignment #1 as a separate homework assignment or just as part of the overall MGRP. There are benefits to both approaches. The benefit to an additional formal assessment is that it might make the bedrock piece stronger. The benefit to leaving it to the final submission is that it encourages the students to be more self-directed in their revisions.

Day 5: The Annotated Bibliography

Objective:

- To touch base with students on the progress of their projects.
- To introduce an annotated bibliography as a useful research tool.
- Introduce the formal annotated bibliography assignment.[9]

Start class with a free write activity on a reflective question: Why do the MGRP? What skills might it cultivate that are useful in other courses or in life? What are you learning about the research process? This free write invites the students to explore how this project is teaching relevant, transferable skills. Additionally, it often reveals that students are pleasantly surprised by how much they are enjoying a research-based project!

- *"Ms. Burns, I actually am enjoying my project. I would never have thought that possible." Karl, senior, project focus: Chris McCandless*
- *Another student emailed Heidi over the night in distress. "Ms. Burns—I think I need to change my topic. I think it's too simple. It's just, well, I'm enjoying my research so much. I think I need a harder topic." Wayland, senior. Heidi's responded to the student's email by saying, "Research shouldn't feel like drudgery. If you're enjoying it, you are most certainly doing something right! This is what research is all about! Not the boring, ho-hum attitude you expressed on the first day of this unit! Isn't it exciting?"*

Understandably, the students' enthusiasm will wane a bit as they tackle the annotated bibliography assignment. Annotated bibliographies are not exciting, and they are a lot of work, but they are an important tool for organizing sources for academic writing. The rest of the class period, therefore, is focused on the less exciting genre of an annotated bibliography.

Most of the students have never created a formal annotated bibliography. They have a vague idea of what it looks like, but most have never used one. With that in mind, Heidi gives a mini-lecture on what an annotated bibliography is and what its purpose to the researcher and reader might be. She talks about the process of gathering and organizing the research in a meaningful way to be used later for the writing process. She also emphasizes the importance of formatting this early on to avoid confusion and frustration later in the process. Heidi tends to end this mini-lecture by showing the students several examples of previously submitted annotated bibliographies.[10]

The next question that naturally arises is "How are we going to cite these sources in our projects?" Student samples again serve a useful role in showing students how various citations are used differently in the various genres.

The academic genre of the background/summary piece requires a formal references page with APA author (date) parenthetical citations. The remaining pieces require a formal bibliography for each piece but not a references page (unless the genre specifically uses one).

This is a great opportunity to discuss reader expectations for the use of sources and citations. In academic writing, the reader expects in-text citations. In most non-academic genres, these parenthetical citations are omitted, but the source material is still credited in some way. Heidi requires that each piece of writing in the MGRP be accompanied by a bibliography, regardless of genre; however, she emphasizes that this requirement is a convention of the academic nature of the overall project, not of the individual genres.

To illustrate, return to the aforementioned project regarding the Battle of the Bulge. In the letter from the soldier to his lover, the student might write, "Lt. Gen. George S. Patton Jr. told us to take some time to celebrate Christmas, so we did!" The student wouldn't use an in-text citation for this information, but he or she would include the source in the bibliography. If this same source were used in the background/summary section, it most certainly would include the author (date) formatting expected of APA documentation. This can be a difficult concept for the students to wrap their minds around. Providing numerous examples of source material in both academic writing and non-academic genres helps.

If possible, have the students open a new Word document. Demonstrate how to format a references/bibliography page, complete with the second-line hanging indent and the alphabetizing tool. Students can then begin creating the first three annotated entries by using the sources from Assignment #1. As the students work on this, the instructor can walk around and check the formatting of these entries and answer questions specific to students' projects.

Note: At this point, students are still spending a large amount of their time researching and not producing much writing. For the last fifteen or twenty minutes of class, encourage students to create a table of contents for their projects. Ask them to identify if all the pieces they're thinking of using (the table of contents entries) fit neatly under the thesis statement they highlighted in the background/summary piece. If not, ask what needs to tweaked (or does anything need to be dumped)? This is an important checkpoint for the unity of their individual projects.

Day 6: A Full Workshop Day: Let's Get Some Writing Done!

Objective:

- To get some writing done

Start Day 6 off with a free write on a reflective question: What are some concerns you still have on the MGRP? Student responses will vary, of course, but in general, at this point, they are beginning to get a good handle on the project and understand the level of effort it will require to successfully complete it.

- *"The Multi-Genre Research Project is a project unlike any I have attempted before. It seems very overwhelming at first with the word count being very high, and how many pieces of writing we are expected to do. I have concerns about being able to finish the project on time." Blaire, freshman, project focus: Joseph Conrad*
- *"I feel that with all of the freedom this project lets me have can be hazardous to the integrity of the project." Chris, sophomore, project focus: Woodstock*
- *"I understand the annotated bibliography part, but how do I differentiate between stuff that I need to cite in my text versus information that just goes on my annotated bibliography?" Connor, sophomore, project focus: Capuchin Monkeys*
- *"I think my biggest concern is time management." Deanna, sophomore, project focus: Disney Parks*
- *"Concerns I have about the MGRP are that I won't have enough time to complete the project. . . . I will have to use my in class time wisely, and make sure I am working on the MGRP as often as possible. I am glad we were given the opportunity to pick our topics, because it makes it more interesting to work on a project that I am fascinated about." Lauren, freshman, project focus: Blackmill Music*

In Heidi's experience teaching the MGRP as a self-contained unit, the students' concerns about time management and scope are recurring from semester to semester. For this reason, Day 6 is devoted mostly to answering student questions and in-class work time. After the free write, engage the students in a conversation of their concerns. Many questions will also be asked about clarification of the project (integrating research and direct quotes, bibliography versus references page, how to cite sources in the bibliography).

Students are often still confused by the difference between the requirement of five pieces of writing and of four different genres. It is useful to reiterate that genres are simply types of writing, and their final MGRP must have a minimum of five pieces of writing that represent four different types (genres) at minimum. This can be a great class discussion, and you will see the students relaxing as their questions and concerns are addressed.

The rest of the class period should be devoted to work time for the students. To make this an effective use of student time, give students directed tips for using the time wisely. Encourage them to really focus on making a plan and getting some work done. Remind them that though they will have a substantial amount of time in class for the project, it will still require time outside of class for completion.

It has been Heidi's experience that this first full work day serves as a deep breath for the students. Most of them will leave the class period with at least two pieces drafted for the final project. Heidi spends the majority of the class period walking around the classroom, engaging directly with the students and their work. It's exciting to see the work they are creating.

Day: 7: Using Books for Research in the MGRP

Objective:

- To give the class an opportunity to visit the library and check out a book that can be used for their research project.

Kevin Kiley (2011), writing for *Inside Higher Education,* cites faculty at the University of Denver in stating that "database research is important to modern-day academics" but researchers "will invariably lose out on serendipitous discovery that comes with perusing a library's stacks" if they fail to address the wealth of information found in the stacks of the library (para. 17).

In informal surveys of her classes over a decade of teaching, Heidi has found that the majority of her first-year composition students have never checked out a book from the university library. While most of these students are freshman, the course often includes upper classmen taking the course late in their academic careers! Most of them express a sense of "who cares about books" or "I just don't know how to navigate the rows of books!" It's especially hard to get technology-savvy students to see value in walking the stacks when they can just sit at their desks and find enough required sources online.

Heidi's experience in the classroom indicates that students are by and large resistant to using books in their research. However, a MGRP asks students to dig deeply into their topics to present new and interesting information that their audience isn't already familiar with. Because books offer a depth of content that most websites don't, it's valuable to teach students how to locate and use books for research.

To make this a hands-on learning experience, plan to take the class on a field trip to the library. Heidi has the students meet in the usual classroom first for a mini-lecture on the value of books in research. This mini-lecture can focus on whatever the instructor wants to highlight, but in Heidi's experience, it's useful to illustrate how books provide a depth of content that other sources can't match.

First, demonstrate to the students how the library book database works and show them how to read the results/records, locate the book location, and check its availability. Additionally, a brief discussion on how the Library of Congress classification system groups books by subject matter teaches the students the value of searching the adjacent shelves in addition to locating a single book.

After walking the students through the online card catalogue, give them five to ten minutes to locate a title relevant to their topics. You will likely need to help them with the keywords. When all the students have a title in hand, walk together to the library and send them off to find their books. Heidi likes to make the checking out of a book the mandatory requirement for the class period. Not surprisingly, most students leave the library with several books in tow—each student as surprised as the next that there are actual books on their topics.

- *"When we went to the library to check out a book, I had low expectations that I could use any of the material only to be pleasantly surprised. The book I choose has an awesome amount of information." Luke, junior, project focus: Joe Mauer*

Students aren't used to turning to books for information, so they are pleasantly surprised when their search is successful. Heidi always has many students comment on their way to the Circulation Desk: "Wow! I had no idea there was a book on my topic!" Mission accomplished.

Day 8: Another In-Class Workday

Objective:

- To introduce the students to types of research materials that aren't limited to the local university library databases or a generalized online search.
- To complete a large amount of research and writing during the workday.

Today is a good day to collect the process folders to see where the students are in the process of compiling their MGRP. It is also a good day to expect the annotated bibliography to be 50 percent complete. Heidi actually has the students turn the partially completed annotated bibliography in for a quick review (she returns both to the students at the end of class).

Because one of the main objectives to the MGRP is the development of strong research skills, Heidi likes to expose the students to as many different research tools as possible. Having already covered library journal databases, online searches, and books, the next type of resources are Google Books for e-books and the Digital Public Library (dp.la)[11] for images. She discusses the different types of content these sources can add to a project and then teaches the students how to navigate the search tools within each site. Finally, she asks students to each locate an e-book and an image to add to their annotated bibliography.

- *"There are so many different resources that I really didn't know existed like Google Scholar and the online books. The resources I'm using are things that I would have overlooked and ignored [before]."* Mariah, junior, project focus: Summer Fashion Forecast
- *"The most surprising thing for me in the process of researching and doing this project is that there's a lot of information to be found throughout the library and different scholarly websites."* Jessica, sophomore, project focus: Eye Color Genetics

The rest of the class period can be allocated for self-directed work time. This is a very busy day for the instructor as you will work individually with students to answer many questions. Try to glance through all the process folders to catch any major "off course" efforts and then immediately conference with the student.

One semester Heidi had a student doing a project on nutrition. The student's annotated bibliography was full of wellness sites selling products and nutrition-supplement/vitamin sites. Heidi was able to talk to the student about quality of and credibility of sources. When the student submitted her annotated bibliography for formal assessment on Day 9, the source list was remarkably stronger. If Heidi hadn't been able to catch the poor source choices in the initial submission, the student would have wasted valuable time or worse, not pursued stronger sources at all.

By now the students have become deeply invested in their topics. It's a fun activity to have "Share what you've learned" breaks. Every ten or fifteen minutes, simply ask if any student wants to share with the class something new and interesting they've learned about their topic from today's research session. In Heidi's experience, there is close to 50 percent participation in each class. An unexpected outcome from the first time Heidi did this (and then in each class thereafter) was that the students began to become engaged in each other's research projects in a way that she hadn't seen before in fourteen years of teaching college composition courses.

Day 9: Final Workshop Day

Objective:

- Reinforce the transferability of the writing skills used in creating a MGRP.

- Self-reflect on the process of writing the formal MGRP.
- Wrap up the writing of the required pieces for the project.

Heidi likes to assign "Learning About Self and Others Through the Multigenre Research Project" by Dickson, DeGraff, and Foard (2002) for Day 9. Assignment #3, a self-reflective piece of writing on the process of writing the MGRP is also due today. Between Dickson et al.'s article and the writing assignment, the students have had some time to really consider how their attitudes toward writing and research have changed over the course of the MGRP Unit. They are beginning to understand that they don't have to know everything about writing to be good at it. They are learning that they need to know *how* to locate the information and analyze the writing situation to be good at writing.

Dickson et al. (2002) write, "Reporting on research [has] often lacked creativity and personal investment" (83). Have the class discuss the idea that writing a conventional research paper is easy but voiceless. A MGRP allows them to merge their voice and their writing to create something that is unique to each of them.

Romano says that good research necessitates a melding of creativity and imagination (Romano, 2000). The students are starting to understand that it's not just about being creative in an artistic sense—it's about being creative in a problem solving, critical thinking sense. Can the researcher see things that somebody else missed? How can they communicate the information in new and engaging ways?

- *"I was surprised at how easily I came up with ideas for the project and how easily it all came together for me. I am excited to see the end result. I have actually learned a lot about my own creativity while working on this project." Olivia, freshman, project focus: Alcoholism*
- *"I'm surprised how fun this project actually is. It is fun to be able to be creative while also providing credible information from scholarly sources." Jacob, junior, project focus: Navy SEALS*
- *"I have learned that I really just have to go for it and once I begin writing the ideas just sort of come to me and it's not a terribly difficult process." Amanda, junior, project focus: Neil Patrick Harris*
- *"I am having a lot of fun displaying my research in different genres. Presenting my information in multiple different genres is helping me organize it more logically." Alli, sophomore, project focus: Athletes and Steroids*
- *"I am enjoying the process. I have fun creating the different pieces of writing and I am proud of the finished products. Presenting my information using different genres allows for more freedom and creativity. I didn't think I was a creative person but this project has shown me that I can be." Katie, sophomore, project focus: Laruen Carlini, volleyball players*

Heidi also uses this opportunity to discuss with the students the transferability of the skills learned in the MGRP. Dickson et al. (2002) talk about how important it is to not allow our pedagogy to be dictated by what our (the professors') academic experience was. For that reason, Heidi reminds the class that teaching a traditional, very structured, research-based conventional essay is actually a whole lot less work for her. It's easy to teach and easy to grade. But, it doesn't teach the skills the students will need in the real world.

Students need to be able to contend with ambiguous writing situations with confidence. They must be able to adapt their writing to different rhetorical situations. They must have the ability to make decisions about genre and style to best meet their communication needs. The MGRP is equipping them with these skills.

Today is a good day to have the students get into groups of five and share their projects in process. Ask them to share their strongest writing piece in the project and their weakest piece. Encourage them to share what they have learned about writing in different genres and what they've learned about their preferences for researching.

- *"The most exciting part of this whole process so far has defiantly [sic] been the research process. I'm usually not the one who likes to research." Caelan, senior, project focus: ISIS Recruitment Strategies*
- *"Different types of writing take very different types of research. I really enjoy writing in different genres because it allows the reader to see different takes on the same subject. Writing in different genres is very refreshing. It is giving me a chance to let more of my voice, opinions, and creativity through." Claire, freshman, project focus: Women in science careers*
- *"The most surprising to me is how fun and exciting this type of project makes research become. I used to hate having to do research paper is because I had to reach a word limit in one type of genre. Spreading the workload over different types of genres has made it surprisingly enjoyable to want to do research." Jayme, freshman, project focus: D-Day, WWII*
- *"I have learned how to be much more flexible with my writing and adapting it to each of the different genres." Mariah, sophomore, project focus: Allyson Felix*
- *"The most surprising part of my research paper is all of the new things that I have learned about Bobby Orr. I am looking forward to more research and what else I can learn." Mac, sophomore, project focus: Bobby Orr*
- *"Writing in different genres is very fun and a great way to explore your writing. I really enjoy it because you can express yourself in different ways and see what you are capable of in your writing." Vito, freshman, project focus: Dave Schultz, Olympic Wrestler*

The students are excited to show off their projects-in-process to their peers. They are proud to be able to competently discuss their research and their writing process. As an observer of the peer discussions, it's hard to not feel a great sense of accomplishment in the students' efforts.

Allow the class to spend the rest of the class period working on the project. If possible, collect the process folders again to catch any remaining issues, noting where sources are needed or remarking on cool pieces in the projects. It also helps see where the students are in the project and who needs a little encouragement to get the project finished on time.

Day 10: The Final Compilation/Proofing Day

Objective:

- To compile the various writing pieces into one final digital file for the students to submit.

"I thought it would take a lot of outside of class time to complete [the MGRP] and that I would get stressed out because of it. However, I found that working in class and putting in a little bit of time outside of class has got me very far in the project. I haven't been stressed out at all." Connor, senior, project focus: Jack Nicklaus

Today is the final work day for the MGRP. Students should have completed all of the required elements of the assignment for the final submission. Today is the day to help them compile all the different pieces of writing into one large document for submission to the Learning Management System for formal assessment and for their presentations.

This day can be handled in any number of ways, depending on how the instructor wants the final projects turned in. Heidi uses this day to teach the students how to use various tools on the computer to turn the document into a Word document and then to save it as a pdf file.

Because the creativity of the students often produces pieces that aren't digital, the students will need to use critical thinking to figure out ways to make their projects digital. It's helpful if the instructor has spent a little time before class becoming familiar with tools like Snip, Paint, print screen, as well as Word functions that allow the insertion of pdf files and pictures.

By the end of the class period, the students should have a complete digital file of their final projects. Heidi has them submit both a digital copy and the hard copy. The assessment occurs on the hard copy and the digital copy is kept to follow up if any questions of plagiarism occur.

Days 11/12: Presentations and Celebration

Because MGRP Unit is the third unit in the semester, the submission for the MGRP is typically at the end of the semester. Heidi blocks out the last two (or three) class periods for a celebration of the process and the semester. The students each give a seven- to ten-minute presentation of their process. Students can either use the digital copy through the SmartBoard or present the hardcopy with the aid of an overhead projector. This is a fun day for the students to show off a finished project that they are really proud of.[12]

Sometimes it is necessary to have the presentations begin a class period before the formal submission due date. In this case, Heidi has the students focus on presenting the process folders if they prefer. Either way, the students are going to be able to share what they learned about their methodology and present in some form the outcome of their research.

Practical Grading Matters

The students will want their projects returned to them. They have devoted hours and hours of their time to this project. They have become invested in the work and are really proud of the finished project. As an instructor, it can be really difficult to get the projects turned around in time to return them to the students before they leave for semester break. This problem can be handled in numerous ways, but one way that Heidi has found to be effective is to have the projects/presentations due on the last two regular class days and then return the assessed projects during finals week.

Heidi has also tried having students submit only the digital copy for assessment, but the students find this disappointing because many of them (in fact, most of them) have put a lot of effort into the tactile presentation of the projects. To respect the extra effort, she does her best to accommodate the submission of the hardcopy.

Some Final Thoughts from the Students

Because Heidi and Michael were able to complete a formal study on the integration of the MGRP into the college classroom, they were able to collect some additional data that further emphasized the students' positive experience when the projects were complete. To conclude the chapter for the self-contained unit, we leave you the words of the students.

Would you recommend the MGRP for future courses?

(A small representative sample of the responses taken from an anonymous survey)

- *"Yes because it was fun and helped teach researching skills."*
- *"Yes! It allows for more passion and creativity."*
- *"Yes. It is much more beneficial than a traditional paper."*
- *"Yes. It has better range for education than a traditional research paper."*
- *"Yes! It really helps students learn how to research and how to relay that information."*
- *"Yes! Provided real-world connections to the writing processes."*
- *"Yes! It was very enjoyable and felt worth taking my freshman year!"*
- *"Yes. It is far more applicable than an eleven-page traditional research paper."*
- *"I would recommend this because it is a far better way to learn writing and research skills in the real world."*

NOTES

1. Heidi usually assigns "The 'Research Paper' in the Writing Course: A Non-Form of Writing" by Richard Larson. While this is an older piece, it reinforces how little has changed in the field of teaching research-based writing.

2. Examples of student MRGPs are available for your classroom use in the online resources for this book.

3. Heidi has included a student-directed genre activity called "Teaching Students about Genres: Writing about the Weather" in the chapter "Plug-In Activities."

4. A sample MGRP Topic Submission Form is available in the appendix.

5. Heidi usually links the class Learning Management System to a couple of online articles that discuss genre. Two in particular that work well are (1) "Investigating Genre: A Micro Version" from the Illinois State University Grassroots Writing Research website and (2) "Genre and Cognitive Development: Beyond Writing to Learn" by Charles Bazerman.

6. The activity, "Teaching Students about Genres: Writing about the Weather" is included in chapter 4, "Plug-In Activities."

7. A detailed assignment sheet for Assignment #1 is available in the appendix. This is a good activity to serve as the bedrock for their MGRP. It outlines the scope and purpose of the project. It is also the easiest piece of writing for the project because it adheres to the expected norms of the informative essay genre.

8. A workshop handout is available in the appendix to be adapted for your use.

9. A formal assignment sheet for the annotated bibliography is available in the appendix for your use to adapt to your classroom.

10. Samples of annotated bibliographies are located within the MGRP in the student samples located in the online sources associated with this book.

11. These two resources are simply suggestions of the author. There are many reputable and valuable databases an instructor can use. The goal is to stretch the students beyond using a general search engine.

12. A formal assignment sheet and rubric for the presentations is available in the appendix for adaption to your classroom.

REFERENCES

Dickson, R., DeGraff, J., & Foard, M. (2002). Learning about self and others through multigenre research projects. *The English Journal*, *92*(2), 82–90. http://doi.org/10.2307/822230.

Kiley, K. (2011, April). No room for books. *Inside Higher Ed.* Retrieved from https://www.insidehighered.com.

Romano, T. (2000). *Blending genre, altering style: Writing multigenre papers.* Portsmouth, NH: Boynton/Cook.

Chapter 3

The Whole Semester Adaptation of the MGRP

As with any other pedagogical approach there are many ways to adapt this method to your own classroom. Examples from Michael's experience will be used to help illustrate the general structure and concepts when using this approach across the entire semester. What follows is the distillation of Michael's experience over the previous six years. Discussions of alternative approaches can be found in other chapters in this book, as well as separate previously published essays and books.

The page number requirement for this project is based on the standard set for Writing Intensive classes. Martha A. Townsend (2001) summarizes standards put forth by various institutions and reveals a range of 2,000–5,000 words as being fairly standard or consistent across various settings.[1] Though her article is over a decade old, these numbers are still the norm being used across the country for public universities. At the schools where Michael has worked, the requirement is 20 pages (250 words per page) or 5,000 words; at least half of the text needs to be commented on by the instructor and revised. It is also important to note that these numbers are minimums, not maximum requirements.

To ensure that students are able to accomplish this task, the writing is broken up into smaller tasks and assignments over the course of the semester.[2] There are two types of writing that students perform throughout the course of the semester when completing a MGRP: short "Easter Egg" papers and installments of their larger project.

"EASTER EGG" PAPERS

First, students have to write small, traditional, research-based papers (so-called "Easter Egg" papers because they require students to investigate and "hunt" for connections to the text). These short (525–700 word) assignments require students to investigate a topic (assigned to them) connected to the exemplar text the class is currently reading. For example, students may be asked to research and write about an event from 1877 and find a connection to Ondaatje's *The Collected Works of Billy the Kid*. Below is an example of the "Easter Egg" paper prompt for that particular book.

For each of these assignments, students are required to use at least two sources, properly document and cite their references, and come to class prepared to share the information they have learned. The reason for these assignments is to ensure that students have the skills to successfully create a piece of basic researched writing. The short papers provide the instructor the opportunity to address basic writing and research skills and to identify additional trends or "quirks" with student writing.

There are also several added benefits with the shorter assignments. First, students have to be able to discern which sources are relevant and accurate to the topic they have been assigned. Second, because they present this information in class, it empowers them to become pseudo-experts on a topic and to teach their peers. Third, the short essays are thesis-driven and as such students have to construct thesis statements that connect abstract subject matter to a

Text Box 3.1   Easter Egg Papers

To encourage discussion and provide each student with material to add to the discussion, there will be seven smaller papers written throughout the semester. Each student will be provided with a topic to research, and then his or her responsibility is two-fold: (1) write a 525–700 word essay about the topic and (2) come to class prepared to teach the class briefly about the topic. This essay should use a minimum of two sources, should provide background about the topic, and should also attempt to make connections to the text that we're currently discussing.

These short essays should be written in 12-point font, Times New Roman or Arial; double-spaced with 1" margins, and include in-text/parenthetical references, and a Works Cited page.

1. Billy the Kid—brief biography
2. *The English Patient* (novel)
3. Brief biography of Michael Ondaatje
4. The Regulators and the Lincoln County War (1877/1878)
5. Ferrotypes
6. 1877
7. 1881

text. Four, these assignments also lessen the page count burden of the MGRP, because the writing demands of the class are being partially met in these shorter assignments.

Finally, the varied connections made by the students reveal the many layers within any particular text. When students realize authors are drawing on historical contexts, or making complex allusions, they see that there is more to a text than words on a page. By hunting for "Easter Eggs" and sharing their findings, students quickly realize how complex even "simple" poems or fiction can be. Understanding this enriches their critical reading skills and also provides examples for them to produce more sophisticated texts of their own.

Typically, Michael includes four or five "Easter Egg" assignments in a given semester. That means half (or nearly half) of the required writing is dedicated to straightforward, research-based, academic writing. This ensures that by the time students have completed the course, regardless of what direction their MGRP takes, they will have necessary transferable skills to perform writing tasks in other classes. It is also an opportunity for students to become comfortable with that particular genre of writing.

This leaves ten pages for students to dedicate to their MGRPs, and, because the "Easter Egg" papers require standardized citation and documentation, it frees students to experiment with other means of giving credit to sources and using sources throughout their project. Sometimes students use footnotes or endnotes, and, as discussed later in this chapter, there is also a required annotated bibliography where students report how and where they use their sources. By allowing students to move beyond formal parenthetical or in-text citations, discussions can be had about how the different forms of documentation affect the reader's experience.

MGRP Installments

The second type of writing students will perform consist of the individual installments of the MGRP. Michael's assignment sheet is intentionally written in a conversational tone to engage students in the project. It begins with a quick introduction, which recaps much of what has already been said about the project in class before this assignment sheet is distributed, and then follows with potential genres for students to investigate and write in. The list of genres is not meant to be exhaustive, but it is meant to show a variety of possibilities and to encourage students to think outside of the forms that might immediately come to mind.

The next part of the assignment sheet outlines the project in greater and more specific detail. Though formally the assignment requires a minimum of only three genres, most students end up contributing four or five before the project is complete. Similarly, even though they have already completed half

MGRP Assignment Sheet, Introduction, and Genre Chart

Introduction

As the name implies, this assignment will require research. That part should be straightforward. You'll have to select a topic that you can find research on, and then figure out how to incorporate it into your larger project. The part that might be causing you to wonder is the "multigenre" part.

But, don't let it scare you. The "multi" part just means, well… multiple. More than one. More than two (since that's a couple). Three, maybe. Maybe four. However many is up to you. The "genre" part, in this case means "form" or "type." So, all it means is that you'll be doing multiple types/forms of writing.

What are some of the forms that you might use? I like to leave it open-ended, but I also understand the need for some examples. So, here goes:

Biography	Obituary	Letters
Police report	Advertisement	Journal article
Greeting card	Diary/journal	To do list
Grocery list	Recipe	Memo
Online chat/IM transcript	Speech	Epitaph
Questionnaire/survey	Note to self/reminder	Interview
Song	Poem	Short story
News article	Novel (or excerpt?)	Textbook (or excerpt?)
Directions	Memoir/Autobiography	Menu
Propaganda	Flyer	Map
Leaflets	Painting	Screenplay (or excerpt?)
Religious materials	Photograph (they're worth 1000 words, right?)	Reference materials (from a dictionary, encyclopedia or something similar)

… and I'm sure there are others. But, that should give you some ideas.

Figure 3.1 MGRP Assignment Sheet, Introduction, and Genre

of the minimum requirements for a writing intensive course (by completing the "Easter Egg" papers), most students exceed the requirement of "5,000 words of your own writing" stipulated on the assignment sheet.

In addition to their own writing, students may also include photos, graphs, charts, maps, interviews, or other work that is not their own to enhance their final project. But, the majority of the project should contain their own writing and work. The key is to provide freedom and flexibility for students to round out the project however they see best fit, while also challenging them to write a cohesive project showcasing their own work.

The final piece of the assignment sheet addresses initial deadlines for the project. An informal proposal is required early in the semester to ensure that students are giving their projects serious thought. It is the beginning of a semester-long "conversation" with their instructor about their projects. Informal writing such as this, and informal conversations in class (or in more formal conferences), provide an opportunity to keep a dialogue going between instructor and student. These conversations, whether in print or

Text Box 3.2 The Nitty Gritty of the Assignment

- By the end of the semester, you will have produced a project that contains at least 5,000 words of your own writing
- However, the final project can (and perhaps should) include things other than your own writing: paintings, drawings, maps, photographs, and perhaps even someone else's writing (newspaper articles, poetry, song lyrics, etc.)
- You must use *at least* three different genres/types/forms in your project. These are not limited to the list above, and if you have any question . . . just ask.
- How you divide the page requirement between the five required assignments is also up to you
- I do require that there is at least one biographic or historical piece that provides an overview of your topic to your reader
- But, the genres/types/forms you choose are entirely up to you
- The **assignment #6** (annotated bibliography) is a part of this project and is really an ongoing assignment, because you will be recording your sources that you've used, how you used them, and why you used them.
- **Your topic** must be "real." By this, I mean you cannot have invented it. You must be able to find research on the topic. It can be a mythical creature like *el chupacabra*, as long as you can find documents that talk about it.
- How are these individual assignments graded? See the rubric on D2L for full details. But, basically, according to four main criteria: (1) quality and use of research; (2) organization, development, and structure; (3) grammar and mechanics; and (4) creativity.

face-to-face, are essential for first-year composition students embarking on such a large project.

For many students, the hardest part of this project is simply coming up with the topic. To help alleviate this stress, Michael likes to have students produce guided lists in an attempt to begin conversations between student and instructor, and between student and student. Students share these lists with one another, ask one another questions about the things on the lists, offer feedback to one another about the items on the lists and fine-tune and narrow the list entries.

The first list that students make is a list of topics. No restrictions or judgments are made about what could appear on the list, so long as it is a potential topic that the student is interested in. Michael likes to encourage lists of at least ten, sometimes more, to push students beyond the obvious, initial ideas

Text Box 3.3   Deadlines

- To get the gears going, you must submit a proposal for the topic that you're considering by **the second week of the semester**. This proposal can be fairly informal. Essentially, I'm looking for about two pages. What topic are you interested in doing? Why? What do you already know about the topic? What kind of genres do you think will work best for this type of project? Why? You can certainly change your topic after that point, but it only makes more work for you. Selecting a topic is important. And, since you'll be working with this topic all semester . . . you'll want to pick something that you are interested in learning and writing about.
- By **the third week of the semester** your first installment is due. This first piece should be something that provides background or an overview of the topic, or an aspect of the topic. A biography, obituary, historical document, newspaper article, or something along those lines works well.
- We will have peer review days, where you bring in your work, share it with others, receive feedback from them, and give them feedback on theirs. So, there will be deadlines for steps of the assignment along the way to make sure everyone has something ready by these days.
- Typically the class period after peer review day will be the day that I collect whichever portion of your project that you're working at that time, so I can grade it and provide feedback of my own.

that spring to mind. Because it is early in the semester and, generally, early in the student's academic career, the lists vary widely. One list could include the following: surfing, genetically modified organisms, photography, Johnny Cash, Roseanne Barr, female comedians, The Clash, medical waste, conspiracy theories, and Ida B. Wells.

Not only do these lists encourage the list maker to generate potential interesting topics, they also inspire learning and conversation between classmates. Each entry on the list represents something that a student knows at least a little about, and that provides an opportunity to be a quasi-expert on the topic with a classmate who knows nothing about that topic. Something one student may have taken for granted as common knowledge, now suddenly is a topic of interest of his or her audience (the classroom).

Once that list is written, shared, and discussed, each student is encouraged to narrow the list to three potential topics. Sometimes this decision is motivated by peer feedback about what is interesting to the group, while other times students already know what topic they really want to explore and are just going through the motions (but even going through the motions at least forces them to consider other possibilities), and sometimes regardless of the amount of lists and discussion, students may change the course of their project midway through the semester.

With the potential topics narrowed, it is now time to generate research questions about each of the topics under consideration. Again Michael tends to go with a list of ten. Students generate ten questions about each of the topics—questions that would guide their research and help them to form thesis statements. Often students get a head start on this list by using some of the questions that their peers ask them when they are sharing their initial list of topics, and sometimes students will return to classmates that they have worked with to help generate ideas for the research questions. Michael always asks for students to share their lists with the whole class and then models how to respond and interact with one another to ensure considerate, but critical, feedback that is constructive to the author and the future of the project.

The next step is to do some initial research and to generate tentative thesis statements. If in a computer classroom, this initial research can be done in class. If not, it can be done as homework. Using this preliminary research, students should be able to generate a list of potential thesis statements. Students can obviously use their own general knowledge to generate the statements, but they should be encouraged to also explore beyond those boundaries.

The final project should reflect what students learned about their topic, not merely what they knew when they began the project. Their knowledge is a starting point, but by encouraging them to push beyond their initial understanding, it demonstrates that research is a process of learning new things— not simply an attempt to affirm or support the knowledge they already have, or assumptions they already believe to be true.

Some of the best projects are based on personal experience or topics that touch a friend or family member. In the past, Michael's students have written about eating disorders (because the student had one, or because a friend did), cancer (because of family history), or even a career choice (based on the student's major, or a parent's job). While these personal connections can certainly help (in terms of direction and primary research), it is important to push students to enhance this knowledge with secondary research. Still, these early research explorations are good opportunities to engage the student's level of comfort with research, documentation, and citation.

As before, students share these lists (of potential topics, of potential thesis statements, etc.). Students pair up, read one another's work, and write or type responses to the peer review questions. Once that is completed, they exchange the feedback, read over what their peer has written, and discuss the feedback. This combination of verbal and written feedback ensures two things. First, it makes sure that each student can read the other's handwriting and understands the points that are being addressed. Second, it provides written feedback for when the students actually sit down to revise their projects.

The peer-sharing helps build a sense of community in the classroom, reveals the diversity of possible topics (and variations within the same topic), and allows for the possibility of sharing material and research on similar projects. Particularly for the college classroom, this sharing reinforces the importance of audience awareness and learning that there are numerous (and acceptable) ways to present information that students may not have considered.

When a draft is due, that class period is dedicated as a workshop day with a structured peer review. Students are given the grade sheet and a handful of questions to help focus their review of one another's work. An example of Michael's peer review questions for the first assignment—one that requires some kind of background or summary—can be found below.

Giving the students the grade sheet ensures that they are familiar with the expectations of the assignment and provides them with an opportunity for self-assessment. The peer review questions are simply a way of initiating a thoughtful conversation about the work at hand. Students are encouraged to create their own questions and to discuss the feedback with their readers.

Again, due to the lack of experience with such projects, it is important to help students set a reasonable pace. To assist with this, the larger MGRP is broken up into six assignments. Each checkpoint (or deadline) provides the student with an opportunity for peer review, feedback from his or her instructor, and a regular interval to ensure progress on the larger project. The number

Text Box 3.4   Peer Review Questions (Assignment #1)

1. Read what they have. Keep in mind: this paper is supposed to provide background or an overview, or an introduction, or a summary, or in some way inform the reader about the topic the larger project will pursue and expand upon. Having read it, how did it do? What are the three things it does best? What three things would you suggest tweaking/changing/improving?
2. What other questions do you have about the topic? Or, to ask another way, what else do you want to know about this topic?
3. Research: does the formatting of the citation and documentation look properly done? If not, what needs to be touched up?
4. Creativity: what would you recommend they do to spice it up? How can they make it more engaging or interesting?
5. Title: offer two suggestions for a title for this section.
6. Thinking ahead to the rest of the project, what would be a section you hope the author includes? And, while you're at it, what is a particular genre that would be interesting to use for this project?

of checkpoints, or deadlines, is completely up to the instructor, but Michael tends toward six.

In a fifteen-week class, this ensures that the students are responsible for some form of formal writing submission every two to three weeks and allows for an opportunity for the instructor to provide feedback or guidance to ensure the project is making progress and not going "off the rails." With the exception of the first and final installment, what students provide in those checkpoint assignments is entirely up to them. Michael encourages them to write substantially so that the burden of page count is distributed more equally across the semester, rather than a burst at the very end.

There are two exceptions to the student-driven content, and those are the first and last installment. The first installment has to be some kind of background (it could take many forms: a historical essay, biography, obituary, overview, etc.) of the subject matter the student has chosen. This is to ensure that the student is beginning with research and attempting to dig into the topic at an academic level. It also proves to be foundational and helps students see the different directions that projects may take. Once the students scratch the surface of research and attempt to write something akin to an encyclopedia entry, they quickly realize what subtopics might interest them and how they might want to revise their research questions.

Because the first installment requires students to take a leap without the benefit of much time to reflect on their projects or to investigate the topics fully, this first "background" piece is often revised dramatically by the end of the semester or scrapped entirely. Students need to be reminded that writing is a cyclical process and that just because they wrote something once doesn't mean that it is complete and finished. This first piece of the project is a perfect opportunity to drive this point home, and often students have the epiphany toward the end of the semester that what they wrote at the beginning no longer fits where they are at the end of the term.

Though it is not preferable for students to change the focus of their topics at this point (due to the amount of work to be redone), occasionally students do change topics mid- or even a late-semester because they find something they are more passionate about. Often it is the background or summary installment of the project that must be jettisoned or redone to accommodate the project's new focus. Sometimes this means the student performs a substantive revision of the first installment, and at other times, it means a complete rewrite with new research. A recent example of this occurred in fall 2015, with a student who wanted to write about cars.

The student began with a history of cars and began narrowing his focus to the Ford Motor Company. On the fourth installment, in November, he wrote a piece about a charity related to Ford. The charity, and his piece about it, sparked conversation in his peer review group and clearly energized the

Table 3.1 Semester-Long Assignment Calendar

				Reading Assignment	Writing (Due)
Aug.	M	24		Bullock (pages 205–213)	
	W	26		Ondaatje (through page 50) // Bullock (pages 1–24)	10 things
	M	31		Ondaatje (finished) // Bullock (pages 52–86)	Egg#1
Sep.	W	2		Ondaatje (afterword)	Proposal
	M	7	No class		
	W	9		Bullock (pages 119–149, and 235–248)	Assignment#1
	M	14		Machiavelli (up to chapter XI)	Egg#2
	W	16	Library	Machiavelli (up to chapter XX)	
	M	21		Machiavelli (finished)	
	W	23		Bullock (pages 164–172)	
	M	28		Exit through the Gift Shop (documentary, in class)	Assignment#2
	W	30		Diaz (up to "Aguantando")	
Oct.	M	5	Online	Diaz (up to "How to Date…") // Bullock (pages 382–386)	Egg#3
	W	7		Diaz (finished)	
	M	12		Bullock (pages 356–365)	
	W	14			Assignment#3
	M	19		Green (pages 9–52)	
	W	21		Green (53–77)	Egg#4
	M	26		Green (4–8)	
	W	28		Green (78–96)	Assignment#4
Nov.	M	2			
	W	4			
	M	9			
	W	11			Assignment#5
	M	16			
	W	18			
	M	23			Assignment#6
	W	25	No class		
	M	30			Presentations
Dec.	W	2			Presentations
	M	7	Final exam		Final MGRP

students around him. The student could have worked the history of the Ford Motor Company into a project that ultimately focused on the charity, but he was so motivated by the new topic that he entirely rewrote the three previous installments and surpassed the page requirement by the end of the class. Obviously, not every student will behave like this one, but from Michael's experience, there is typically one per semester that does.

In addition to the peer reviews and discussions, Michael also requires that students perform formal reflections on each installment of the students' projects. Text Box 3.4 has some examples for reflection questions.

Text Box 3.4 Reflection Questions

For each piece, answer the following questions:
1. What am I saying here?
2. How does what I am saying here contribute to the larger project?
3. What genre am I using here? Why do I think this particular genre is best suited for this type of information? What does this genre expose about the topic or what about this genre is best suited to deliver this information?

And then for the project as a whole, answer the following:
1. How many pages have you currently written? And how many pages do you have left to go to meet the basic requirements of the assignment?
2. How many genres have you used? And how many do you have left to go to meet the basic requirements of the assignment?
3. What else do you have to say about this topic?
4. What's the best way (form/genre/type of writing) to say it?
5. What do you need help with?
6. What questions do you have with regard to the expectations of the remaining semester?

Michael has the students formally submit these reflections for assessment and accountability. These periodic checks require students to ensure they are on track with their projects and require students to be aware of how and why they are doing what they are doing. Sometimes as part of the reflective process, students are required to perform a "reverse outline" to better "see" their projects, and this set of reflective questions is essentially another form of doing just that.

The final installment is an annotated bibliography. Michael allows students to choose the form of citation that they use throughout their essay; they can use footnotes or endnotes or in-text or parenthetical citations, but at the end of the project, all students must include an annotated bibliography that performs three tasks. First, it must provide an alphabetized, properly formatted list of sources. Second, it will include short summaries (two to three sentences) for each source. Third, it will indicate where and how students used each source. For this criterion, Michael encourages students to direct the reader to specific pages or sections of the source.

In between installments one and six, the content, genre, and page count are all up to the students. This places the burden of progress on them and makes each student his or her own project manager. It relieves the instructor of keeping count or tabs on what has or hasn't been submitted and instead allows the instructor to become more of a coach and collaborator. The focus then for the instructor is to provide critical feedback, suggestions, and to ask probing questions about how this fits into the larger scope of the project. In short, the instructor becomes more of a class peer modeling peer review than a taskmaster.

THE TEXTS

It is important to provide students with a variety of texts for a class that teaches them to write in a variety of styles. Michael's approach is to offer three types of texts: a writing guide (he prefers the *Norton Field Guide to Writing*, because it is arranged according to genre), exemplars (in short, professionally published works that model the multigenre approach), and student examples. The hope is that in providing students with a variety of writing tools, they will be better equipped to make intentional choices about their own writing.

Student examples are readily available online, but it is better to be able to draw from previous student projects with which an instructor is familiar. This can be difficult if it is your first time using the approach, simply because you have no previous student work to draw from, but the solution is simple: create your own MGRP. Yes, it takes work, but in doing so, you will become much more familiar with the task you're asking your students to undertake, and you will be better prepared to anticipate where they may stumble along the way.

In addition, assuming you choose to reveal to your students that you wrote the project, students thoroughly enjoy the opportunity to see your writing and to critique it. More importantly, because you will have written it, you will be intimately familiar with the subject matter, the research that went into it, and how and why it was constructed the way it was. These are essential components for understanding and teaching the multigenre project.

Choosing exemplar texts, as with choosing text for any class, is often a matter of preference. Fortunately, there are many books (novels, poetry collections, comic books, graphic novels, and films) that employ the multigenre approach. The book suggested by Romano, and other proponents of the MGRP, is Michael Ondaatje's *The Collected Works of Billy the Kid* (1970). This book is a collection of poetry, nonfiction, interviews, short fiction, photographs, etc. Though it is a somewhat complicated text, with a little work students are able to engage and appreciate it.

A useful tool for teaching this book is Ondaatje's afterword that is included in the 2008 edition and is available online. In this afterword, the author discusses the process he used to create the text. He addresses starts and stops, struggles and difficulties, and the focus and direction that ultimately led him to finish the book in the manner that he did. This reflective piece is both useful for understanding *The Collected Works of Billy the Kid*, and for modeling reflective, self-aware analysis of writing which students might want to emulate in their own projects.

If Ondaatje's work doesn't appeal, then there are plenty others to choose from. Several teachers have mentioned the possibility of using Sharon M. Draper's *Tears of a Tiger* (1994, 1996) and/or Avi's *Nothing But the Truth* (1992).[3] These texts are geared more toward a younger audience, but each text can still challenge college readers. Sections of both of these texts are written in email format or memos or notes, etc., and so they also model the multigenre approach.

In teaching texts like these, the focus is really on the structure of the work and the choices made by the author. So rather than memorizing plot points or character names, students should focus instead on why the author chose to portray an event in a poem rather than a short piece of fiction, or include a photograph and a description of the person, or why text messaging might be the most effective means of communicating a point. The attention shifts from the traditional gaze (plot, character, setting) taught in the classroom, to a critique of form, genre, and technique.

Of course, it is not necessary to use a book that mirrors the MGRP approach. Choices can be made to include books of different genres (poetry, fiction, short stories, a collection of interviews, etc.). When reading these texts, students would focus on better understanding this particular form and analyzing how each form works. The intention of using a multigenre book or of using various stand-alone texts is to encourage discussions surrounding questions like: what are these genres most effective for and what rules govern that particular genre?

Michael frequently partners Ondaatje's book with a short story collection, a comic book (or graphic novel), and Niccolo Machiavelli's *The Prince*. There are plenty of choices for the short story collections. Michael tends to use Ernest Hemingway's *The Snows of Kilimanjaro and other stories* (the title story was Hemingway's favorite of his work and has other iconic Hemingway short stories in the collection).

Similarly, there are many choices for comic books or graphic novels. Michael has successfully used Justin Green's *Binky Brown meets the Holy Virgin Mary* (1972), Debbie Drechsler's *Daddy's Girl* (1995, 2008), and Robert Triptow's *Class Photo* (2015). These books work well because they are nontraditional comics, are self-contained, and they experiment with the genre of comic art. It should be noted that all deal with adult themes (*Binky Brown* deals with masturbation and obsessive-compulsive disorder, *Daddy's Girl* deals with incest and rape, and *Class Photo* has a variety of adult situations, though typically humorous and not as stark as *Daddy's Girl*).

Regardless, providing an example of sequential art allows students to see the possibility of how text and images complement one another.

Michael's choice to include *The Prince* is motivated by two desires. First, it is a complicated, often-cited, or alluded-to text that challenges students to think critically as they read, which results in rich classroom discussions. Second, and more apropos, it is first and foremost a "how to" book. The very idea that someone would write an instructional manual about how to rule a kingdom (among other topics) is eye-opening to students and poses new possibilities for the process genre. This book can be paired with Junot Diaz's short story "How to Date a Brown Girl (Black Girl, White Girl, or Halfie)" in order to generate unique student process essays (see assignment on page 68).

Regardless of the choices of texts, it is important to remember the focus of composition is on writing and not analyzing literary texts. The emphasis should be placed on deconstructing the text, identifying the rules that govern the genre, and understanding the rhetorical situations each form is most effective for addressing. For these reasons, a wide variety of texts can be used in this type of classroom setting—highbrow, lowbrow, young adult, any number of the colloquially termed "genre" novels (romance, sci-fi, fantasy, etc.).

Not only are these texts an opportunity to provide models for students, they also help break up the course and provide opportunities for discussion. As students become more self-aware about their own writing, they will begin to notice more nuances within the writing of others.

CONCLUSION

Like any new approach used in the classroom, a lot of trial and error is involved in perfecting the use of the MGRP, but the rewards for student and instructor are great. Not only does the project help achieve the objectives of first-year composition (as outlined in chapter 1), but, due to the collaborative spirit of the classroom outlined above, it also ensures a sense of community with students and encourages students to engage their instructors directly.

While the texts, deadlines, number of installments, number of genres, number of pages or word count, and thematic freedom may vary from class to class and instructor to instructor, ultimately the scholarship reports (again and again) increased satisfaction and engagement on the student and instructor level. By allowing intellectual creativity into the classroom, students develop a better sense of the diversity of writing possibilities and the rules that govern them, and instructors end up with final projects that they actually want to read at the end of the semester.

NOTES

1. Primarily pages 247–248.
2. This is also in keeping with the "best practices" put forth by Writing Intensive class standards and addressed by Townsend (248–249).
3. For example, Nancy Mack in *Engaging Writers with Multigenre Research Projects* (2015), 3.

REFERENCE

Townsend, M. A. (2001). Writing intensive courses and WAC. In S. H. McLeod, E. Miraglia, M. Soven, & C. Thaiss (Eds.), *WAC for the new millennium: Strategies for continuing WAC programs* (pp. 233–258). Urbana, IL: NCTE.

Chapter 4

Plug-In Activities

INTRODUCTION

One of the exciting things about the multigenre research project (MGRP) is the diversity of work that students are producing. One of the challenges is that when you have twenty-five students working on different projects and topics, it can be hard to find in-class activities that are relevant to everyone. Not every student project will require a short story, poem, graph, or other specific genre.

One of the broader goals of the MGRP is to expose students to different genres and to explore the rhetorical choices that accompany different genres. Because students will encounter any number of types of writing in their futures (graduate school, workplace, etc.), exposing students to a wide variety of genres is in their best interest. Additionally, and more directly applicable to their work in class, by examining numerous forms, identifying the grammar or rules of those forms, and working within those constraints, students will become more aware of the rules, restrictions, and freedoms allowed within their preferred genres. It is with these ideas in mind that the activities in this chapter are constructed.

What follows this short introduction are in-class activities that the authors have found particularly effective in the classroom. The discussions that ensue after completing the activities are productive and have helped students to think critically of the variety of genres available to them, why and when they may use them, and how to better navigate this type of writing when they encounter it (whether it be in a textbook, an academic journal, the workplace, etc.). These activities are not all inclusive. They should be used as a launching point for the activities that best fit the tenor of your specific classroom.

As a general rule, any text could be used in a classroom activity. We have used a variety of fiction, nonfiction, essays, former student work (with permission), newspapers, letters, recipes, photographs, and maps. The important thing to remember when using such texts is that the text itself is not as important as the form is and what students can learn from it. This involves asking questions directly relevant to the projects that students are creating. What are the bare essentials of this form? How does it differ from other genres that fall under the bigger umbrella of "literature"? What rhetorical choices did the author have to make for this form to be effective? How is the message more effectively conveyed through this form than, say, poetry or an essay? In some cases, it might be important to discuss the overall theme of a text, but the caution is to stay focused on the form and not allow the content to become the focus of the lesson.

There is always a danger when teachers provide students with examples, or break down complicated tasks into simple steps, that students will simply latch onto that example (or process) to produce their own work. It is essential to remind students that just because they like a particular form or genre, it does not mean that that genre will fit within the confines of their project. It is for these reasons that the discussions about "when and why this genre can be effective" are particularly important. It is also why, particularly at the beginning of the MGRP (whether it be a unit or a full class adaptation), it is important to showcase and demonstrate a variety of genres. This chapter provides useful examples to aid in this endeavor.

PLUG-IN ACTIVITY 1: ANALYZING GENRE: USING NEWSPAPERS IN THE CLASSROOM

Objective
To help students better understand genre and the rules that govern different genres

Approximate Time Required: 60 minutes

Materials Needed
- Newspapers: Enough for each student to one and ideally three to four different publications

Rationale
Students benefit from concrete examples of genre. This activity pushes students to see the rules that govern the form rather than simply being observers of the information. By asking students to read newspapers and interpret for themselves the set of rules/expectations for that form, it encourages them to think critically about the type of writing they are reading and not just the information provided within the writing. Students benefit from being able to identify the different structures, forms, uses of citation, etc., and then to apply how those conventions work within the argument that the writing is presenting. In doing so, they will better understand why an understanding of genre and its various forms is valuable to strong communication. This activity, as with almost every example in this book, reinforces discussions of audience, purpose, and rhetorical situation.

What to do before class
Provide some cursory research about the audience of each of the newspapers that you'll be using in class and construct a list of your own rules/expectations for newspaper writing. Michael has included a list that may be helpful below.

What to do during class
First, have students flip through their assigned newspaper and acquaint themselves with it. In Michael's experience, he finds this is often one of the first times a student has ever actually sat down with a newspaper. They've read news before, but in fits and starts or online. It's rare that he has encountered a student who has actually read through a paper in its entirety.

Next, have students work to identify the target audience of the paper. It's helpful to provide a list of criteria to guide this analysis. Here are a few questions that Michael finds useful: What topics does the newspaper cover? Is there (for example) a dedicated sports page, or is it simply part of another section of the paper? Are the stories local, national, international, or a mixture? Is there a consistent focus throughout? Who can afford the products that are advertised? How many images are included? Are the images color or black and white? How big is the font that's used? What type of political bias is present in the news? What topics are covered in the op-eds? How much does the paper cost? What's the paper called?

With the audience in mind, have students now group up with other students who have the similar publication. As a group, they should choose some articles and investigate them more carefully with an eye to structure, tone, format, use of sources, etc.

Each group should then share information about their paper and what they discovered with regard to the conventions of newspaper writing.

As a class, it is helpful then to compile a list of these expectations. Given the variety of papers used, it should be easy to find overlap between them.

What to do after the activity
Have students take an essay they've written for another purpose (it could even be from another class) and revise it into a newspaper-appropriate format.

List of newspaper genre conventions
- First, know your subgenre (editorial, expose, feature, informative/newsbeat, etc.). Each of these has different expectations and rules.
- Newspaper articles are front-loaded—meaning they provide a complete summary up front. The lede: who, what, when, where, how, and why.
- The lede should contain one main idea, make clear what the story is about, and be exciting or reveal tension
- Cut extraneous words
- Shorter sentences: generally twenty-five words or fewer
- Don't use "I"
- Generally in the past tense
- Full name and title when first mentioning someone and then last name after that *Example: Colonel Roger Clemens, initially, and simply Clemens thereafter.*
- To assert authority/credibility, the title (or qualifications) of the source is indicated. *Example: Heidi Burns, instructor at Minnesota State University, teaches a multigenre research paper in lieu of a traditional-research paper to better meet the core learning objectives of most ENG 101 programs.*
- Emotion: pathos is a powerful motivator, but it also hooks readers. Often this comes in the form of carefully chosen quotations or reactions from witnesses.
- Most important . . . least important. Start with the most important and work your way to the least important piece of information. Think of your

newspaper-appropriate revision as being structured like a funnel: you start out broad with all the most important information and then wind your way down to more and more specific, detailed information. It's all relevant, but ultimately the reader should know what he or she needs to know after the first paragraph, and the other paragraphs will only add to his or her understanding of the topic.

PLUG-IN ACTIVITY 2: AUDIENCE AWARENESS ACTIVITY: LET'S RAISE THAT TUITION!

Objective
To make students aware of rhetorical choices that must be made to communicate with different audiences.

Approximate Time Required: 30 minutes

Materials Needed:
None

Rationale
Students sometimes have a hard time understanding that they are writing for an audience, not just an instructor. They don't take into account the target audience or the egocentrism of audience members. This activity works to illustrate to students how one purpose can have numerous audiences and how the message must be adapted and tailored to each specific audience if the writer is to successfully communicate with the intended audience.

What to do before class
Determine what topic you're going to use for the students to write about. For illustrative purposes, this activity is going to use the topic of raising tuition with the purpose of persuading the intended audience that a tuition increase is a good idea.

What to do during class
Break the students into four groups. Explain that the entire class has the same purpose, but each group will have a different intended audience. The students will first perform an audience analysis for their assigned audience, consider supporting details that are relevant to the assigned audience, consider counterarguments, and finally, create an outline for their argument.

First, assign an audience to each group.

- Group 1—Audience: Students attending the college. Purpose: To persuade my audience that tuition increases are a good idea.
- Group 2—Audience: Parents of students attending the college. To persuade my audience that tuition increases are a good idea.
- Group 3—Audience: Faculty at the college. To persuade my audience that tuition increases are a good idea.
- Group 4—Audience: Administration at the college. Purpose: To persuade my audience that tuition increases are a good idea.

Next, using a handout or a SmartBoard slide, have the students use the following questions to analyze their audiences:

1. What are the general characteristics of my audience (age, education level, values)?
2. What is their personal investment in the cost of tuition at this college?
3. What impact will a rise in tuition have directly on this audience?
4. What sorts of things would this audience be interested in that might result from increased tuition dollars?
5. Why might this audience be opposed to a tuition increase?

Finally, provide a guideline for structuring the argument. A potential outline format could be:

Title:

Purpose:

Thesis statement:

Introduction: Attention getter

Supporting main point #1:

Supporting main point #2:

Supporting main point #3:

Address counterargument #1:

Address counterargument #2:

Conclusion statement:

What to do after the activity
Have each group share with the class what qualities they took into account when determining the values and attitudes of their assigned audience. As a class, discuss which of the characteristics are more important to the specific purpose at hand. Next, have the students share their arguments. Again, as a class, dissect the arguments to determine points where the group did a good job of tailoring the message to their intended audience and places where they could have done a stronger job. Finally, compare how the values and attitudes

of the four different target audiences vary widely, requiring different supporting arguments, but how they all ultimately carried out the same purpose of persuading the audience that tuition increases are a good idea.

PLUG-IN ACTIVITY 3: EVALUATING WEBSITES FOR SOURCE MATERIAL: IS IT CRAAP OR CRAP?

Objective
Students tend to turn to the internet first and foremost for their secondary source material. Unfortunately, most students don't approach the internet with the critical thinking skills they need to assess whether a website is a strong source for their research needs. Consequently, they use poor sources to support and develop the content in their writing. Teaching students how to quickly determine the credibility and usability of online sources will strengthen their source material and help them produce stronger content.

Approximate Time Required: A minimum of 30–40 minutes.

Materials Needed
An assessment worksheet

Rationale
There are many ways to teach students to evaluate websites, but most of the methodologies involve some variation of an acronym (CRAP, CAARP, CABLE, CARP, etc.). As an instructor, you can choose whichever acronym fits the personality of your classroom. The goal is to make it memorable for the students. CRAAP is this author's preference because it allows the students to ask themselves the question, "Is this website CRAAP or is it simply crap?" Just be sure the acronym addresses in some way the criteria of authority, accuracy, purpose, bias, reliability, and currency.

While this activity could easily be accomplished outside of the classroom as homework assignment, the benefit to devoting class time to it is noteworthy. The instructor can engage the students in conversations about why or why not different websites are good sources. The instructor can answer general questions for immediate feedback. This will result in the students taking the time to locate and document stronger sources for the formal assessment of the activity.

What to do before class
Prepare a website analysis worksheet to reflect the acronym of your choice (or use the one provided below "Evaluating a Web Source: Is it CRAAP or is it crap").

What to do during class
Using a SmartBoard, perform a basic web search for the class to model. It helps to choose a topic that is relevant to the students' current writing

assignment. In the case of the MGRP, ask one of the students to identify the topic of his or her project. Walk the students through the initial search results.

Teach the students to eliminate any URLs with a "wiki" tag, "about.com" tag, or any number of blog tags (wordpress.com, blogspot.com, ehost.com, godaddy.com, etc.). Remind students that anybody can post things online. Heidi likes to use the example of a seventh grade class posting research papers online. A brief discussion on why these types of sources don't meet the criteria for academic writing should include the questions of authorship and reliability.

Next, locate a source that seems reliable from the URL and click on it. Then take the students through the process of identifying the various qualifiers for a credible website. If the students are unable to verify the source's credibility through the provided acronym, briefly discuss why the source shouldn't be used for academic writing and return to the search results for another example.

It's especially useful if the instructor can locate a source that appears legitimate but cites the source of its content as Wikipedia at the bottom of the page. This reinforces to the students the importance of walking through the entire validity test before relying on the content for secondary source material in their own projects.

After the instructor has successfully modeled the evaluation of several sources (with a mix of credible and non-credible), pass out the worksheet and have the students locate four websites that are applicable to their own projects and assess the credibility of said sources. This is a good time for the instructor to walk around the classroom and have conversations with students about the various websites they are encountering.

What to do after the activity

Reinforce the necessity of using strong supporting materials in academic writing. Encourage students to add the websites they've located and verified as credible to their annotated bibliographies for inclusion in the formal MGRP.

SAMPLE WEBSITE ANALYSIS WORKSHEET

Evaluating a Web Source: Is it CRAAP or is it Crap?
For this activity, you are going to locate and evaluate four web sources. You will need to copy and paste this page to reflect the four sources you evaluate. When you are finished, please submit to the appropriate dropbox for assessment.

Name of the website you are evaluating:

URL of the website:

Keywords used to locate this website:

Using the acronym CRAAP, why is this a good source or a poor source choice for your project?

C: Currency: What is the most recent date associated with the website? Is it current enough to be used in your project? Is it updated frequently?
R: Reliability: Is the page mostly free of advertisements? Does the website cite other sources for its information? Is it written for an academic audience?
A: Authorship: Can you identify clearly who the author is (whether it is a person or an organization)? Is this a well-known author or a respected organization in the field?
A: Accuracy: Is the information free of grammatical errors? Does the information complement the other research you've encountered?
P: Purpose: Why does the website exist? Is it to inform or to sell you something? Is it tied to a major industry or is it educational in purpose? Is there bias present that needs to be addressed?

Overall assessment: I believe this website is **credible/not credible** for the following reasons (briefly describe).

If the website is credible and useful for your project, please create an APA source entry here and then copy and paste it into your formal annotated bibliography for inclusion in the final MGRP.

PLUG-IN ACTIVITY 4: TEACHING STUDENTS ABOUT GENRE: WRITING ABOUT THE WEATHER

Objective

To analyze a rhetorical situation, research an assigned genre and create a brief piece of writing that is appropriate to each groups' assigned audience, genre, and purpose.

By the end of the activity, students will be able to:

- Apply the specific conventions of an assigned genre to a piece of writing
- Integrate source material into their assigned genre
- Explain the different rhetorical choices made for their assigned genre, purpose, and audience
- Begin to understand the concept of unity in the MGRP

Approximate Time Required: 35 minutes

Materials Needed
Five notecards with five related topics, each addressing a different audience and purpose

What to do during class
Divide the class into five equal groups. Assign each group a genre by giving them one notecard. Tell them they all have the same topic: "March is the snowiest month of Minnesota," but they all have different genres, audiences, and purposes. They are to research the conventions of their assigned genre, research the information necessary to write a non-fiction piece of writing about March being the snowiest month in Minnesota, and then create a piece of writing to share with the class. When they present their writing to the class, each group will explain the conventions of their assigned genre and the rhetorical choices they made to meet their assigned purpose and audience's expectations.

Tell the students they are allowed to be creative with their writing, but all the information in it must be based on researched facts (i.e. if they are writing about a car accident resulting from poor visibility on March 13 on a certain highway, they need to be able to prove the weather was actually bad that day and that the highway exists).

Group 1: Genre: Email Alert
Audience: Viewers of the local weather news station
Purpose: to inform viewers of a winter warning

Group 2: Genre: Memo
Audience: K-12 teachers and staff
Purpose: To inform the staff of school policy for weather-related early releases

Group 3: Genre: Police Report
Audience: the police officers
Purpose: to report on a weather-related accident

Group 4: Genre: News Article
Audience: *The Reporter* readers in local readership area
Purpose: to inform the readers about a weather-related incident in the area

Group 5: Genre: Obituary
Audience: attendees at a funeral
Purpose: to celebrate the life and death of Mankato resident related to bad weather

What to do after class
After each group has presented their findings on their assigned genres and their pieces of writing, ask them if all of the writings could exist in a formal submission for this MGRP. A discussion of "the unity of the writings" will, which is very helpful for students to understand how unity across genres can be achieved. In most cases, you will find the students immediately say that yes, the writings are all related because they're all about weather in Minnesota. The goal is to help them understand that while the topic is the same, the piece of writing aren't related to each other in any other way. A unified MGRP might have the same diversity of genres, but the content of each pieces of writing needs to lead directly into the next piece in some way.

To illustrate this point, Heidi goes back to the five topics. She shows how the topics could reach unity if each of the pieces of writing were related in this one (this is just one of many possible examples):

Genre 1: Kare 11 report about bad weather coming to Minnesota
Genre 2: School Memo letting teachers know of an early release
Genre 3: Police report of a two-car accident near a local school
Genre 4: Newspaper article covering the death of a local principal
Genre 5: A funeral obituary of the principal

Of course, it's important to note in this particular example, Heidi is using a fictitious person and incident. In the case of the formal submission of the MGRP, the content will be based on real incidents, people, and places.

PLUG-IN ACTIVITY 5: WRITING A "HOW-TO": TEACHING THE PROCESS GENRE

Objective

To engage students in an exploration and understanding of an often overlook genre: the process genre. By the end of this activity, students should be able to:

- Showcase an array of possible uses for an overlooked genre,
- Discuss how and why the authors use this form and what is gained from its use,
- Identify the essential elements of the process genre and its strengths and weaknesses, and
- Create their own "how to" piece of writing.

Approximate Time Required: 75 minutes

Materials Needed
Four examples of process writing

Rationale
Students do not typically appreciate how versatile the "how to" form is. In order to explore the numerous possibilities the form allows, Michael typically has students read three or four of the following: Junot Diaz's short story "How to Date a Brown girl (Black girl, White girl, or Halfie)," a narrative recipe (Michael likes Alton Brown or Ree Drummond, aka the Pioneer Woman, and sometimes use my own recipe for Jack Daniel's Chocolate Chip Cookies), the entry for "How to Take a Shower" from the WikiHow webpage, and Paul McHenry Roberts' essay "How to Say Nothing in 500 words." Each of these texts provides unique insight into the process genre and results in interesting discussions about the form.

 Diaz's short story uses the "how to" form to address racial stereotypes and dating, things not typically thought of when students consider the process genre. Narrative recipes, as the name implies, tell a story (typically explaining the "why" behind each step) along with the necessary instructions to construct a dish. The WikiHow page poses interesting questions for consideration such as: If you didn't know how to take a shower would you have the know-how to turn on a computer and find this page? If you are unfamiliar with showering, is this instructional guide really complete enough or are there steps missing? Finally, Roberts' essay speaks directly to the art of writing and addresses many of the foibles that students fall prey to.

What to do before class
Make copies of the four texts available for students. Each student will need access to all four texts. You can either create digital links in the Learning Management System, or you can make hard copies.

What to do during class
Begin by having students read all of the selected texts before class. Next, divide the students into small groups and assign each group one of the texts. It's important that all students are familiar with all of the texts to some degree, but it also valuable for students to become quasi-experts on a single text and to be able to speak about it in detail. Allow 10 minutes for students to re-read and refresh their memories about the text for which they are responsible. The goal of this discussion is to identify the effectiveness (strengths and weaknesses) of each text: what works, what doesn't, and what is missing?

After each group has identified the effectiveness of the assigned texts, have the students make an outline of the text; this can happen as a small group activity where each small group creates an outline to share with the larger group or this outline could be created as a class discussion with the outline being written on the board. Once the basic framework of the texts have been identified, they can be compared to identify the commonalities, or traits, of the process genre.

To wrap up the activity, assign a short writing assignment. Give the students 10 or 15 minutes to draft their own "how to" piece that is related to their individual MGRP. Though it may be a stretch, almost every topic students will select includes some process that could be explored. For example, if the topic is cancer treatment, either the spread of the disease or surgical removal could easily be explained in a process essay. A favorite student example born from this activity is a recipe for the trilateral commission (included in the online sources associated with this book).

What to do after the activity
Encourage students to share these "how to" essays. Ask them to reflect on the different rhetorical choices each student had to consider relevant to the topic matter and the purpose of their unique pieces of writing.

Suggested Resources
Diaz, J. (1995, December 25). How to date a brown girl (black girl, white girl, or halfie). *The New Yorker*, 88.

Drummond, R. (2015). The Pioneer Woman [Web page]. Retrieved from http://www.thepioneerwoman.com.

The Food Network. (2015). Alton Brown [Web page]. Retrieved from http://www.foodnetwork.com/chefs.

Roberts, P. (1958). How to Say Nothing in Five Hundred Words. In *Understanding English* (pp. 403–422). New York: Harper.
How to take a shower. (2015). Wikihow [Web page]. Retrieved from http://wikihow.com.

PLUG-IN ACTIVITY 6: INFOGRAPHIC MAKING

Objective

To encourage the use of charts, graphs, maps, and other infographics in student writing.

Approximate Time Required: 30 minutes

Materials Needed
- A computer with access to the internet and access to the video "Kurt Vonnegut on the shapes of stories" available in a number of online locations, including: https://vimeo.com/53286941 or https://www.youtube.com/watch?v=9-84vuR1f90.
- It helps if the class has access to a computer lab or their own laptops, but this can be done as a handwritten activity also.

Rationale

Just as photographs can convey complex ideas efficiently, so too can graphs, charts, maps, and other infographics. Students tend toward citing statistics and cluttering their writing with attempts to regurgitate difficult source material. Though summary and paraphrase should certainly be encouraged, having students create a graph, chart, map, or other infographic is a creative way to encourage them to employ the skills of summary and paraphrase without their realizing that's what they're doing. In order to create a unique infographic, students need to have conducted research and have the ability to understand what they've read and find a pattern (or sense of organization) in the material. Not only are these infographics insightful and useful to liven up a MGRP but they are also deceptively complex to create (but very rewarding when completed).

What to do before class

If you're conducting the activity in a computer lab, then familiarize yourself with infographic-making software that you can recommend to students. Excel, Numbers, Google Docs, and similar spreadsheet programs work well, but there are also plenty of free webpages that offer unique features.

If you are completing this activity outside of a computer lab, then it helps to bring examples of infographics to give students ideas for creating their own. Additionally, be sure to have plenty of paper available, markers, and any other tools that you think will be helpful.

What to do during class

Show Kurt Vonnegut's video about charting stories. It's funny, but it also provides an example of a creative chart/graph that might not immediately come to mind for students. Ask students how Vonnegut's chart was effective? What ways could we improve his chart? What effect does it have when we combine a "creative" art with a "scientific" form (such as a chart/graph)?

The hope is to inspire students to think more creatively about the options available to them. Charts and graphs don't need to merely contain statistics and figures, and they don't need to only accompany reports. Infographics can concisely and efficiently convey complex information to the reader and often become a showpiece of a MGRP. It's also important to remind students that the information within the infographic needs to be properly cited, and they should complete a References page to accompany their work.

What to do after the activity

Have students share their infographics with one another. Not only does this sharing provide the opportunity to "show off" but it also helps to ensure that the infographic is understandable and conveys the information the author intended. An additional benefit is that students will see the diversity of approaches and techniques that can be used.

Suggested Resources

The following is a list of some free applications to create infographics (it is by no means exhaustive):

- Canva: https://www.canva.com/
- Charts—Google Developers: https://developers.google.com/chart/
- Dipity: http://www.dipity.com/
- Easelly: http://www.easel.ly/
- Infogram: https://infogr.am/
- Photo Infographic Gen Lite: https://play.google.com/store/apps/details?id=mariusSoft.InFotoFree&hl=en
- Piktochart: http://piktochart.com/
- Venngage: https://venngage.com/
- Visme: http://www.visme.co/
- Visually: http://visual.ly/

Additionally, there are a number of good books that discuss how to use and how to create infographics. The McClure and Toth (2015) article, especially, is thoughtfully constructed and provides important questions to ask about authority and credibility with regard to charts, graphs, and infographics in general. The Lankow, Richie, and Crooks (2012) book provides a solid foundation for understanding infographics. The Doyle (2013) book is not a "how to" book by any means but rather a collection of insightful and creative infographics. Finally, Smith's (2014) text is a children's book, but it takes very complicated (particularly large and hard to visualize topics) and resizes them in imaginative ways that might inspire students.

Doyle, P. (2013). *World War II in numbers: An infographic guide to the conflict, its conduct, and its casualties*. Richmond Hill, Ontario: Firefly Books Ltd.

Lankow, J., Ritchie, J., & Crooks, R. (2012). *Infographics: The power of visual storytelling*. Hoboken, NJ: Wiley.

McClure, H. & Toth, C. (2015). Louder than words: using infographics to teach the value of information and authority. In P. Bravender, H. A. McClure, & G. Schaub (Eds.), *Teaching information literacy threshold concepts: Lesson plans for librarians* (pp. 166–172). Chicago, IL: Association of College and Research Libraries.

Smith, D. J. (2014). *If. . . A mind-bending way of looking at big ideas and numbers*. Tonawanda, NY: Kids Can Press Ltd.

PLUG-IN ACTIVITY 7: LIBRARY SCAVENGER HUNT

Objective

To familiarize students with the library resources and to showcase the diversity of materials at their disposal. By the end of this activity, students should be able to:

- Locate a variety of library materials,
- Operate the moveable stacks in the library,
- Document a print source in APA format, and
- Check out a book from the library.

Approximate Time Required: 60 minutes

Materials Needed
- List of items students need to locate and document

Rationale

Because of the ease and ubiquity of the internet, students need to be reintroduced to the library and made aware of the variety of sources available to them. Heidi and Michael typically create a list of nine items students need to locate on their scavenger hunt. The list consists of items from each floor of the library and various available materials or resources (government documents, books, games, DVDs, art, maps, etc.). By highlighting items students might not generally associate with the library, this activity causes students to re-evaluate what the library does have to offer.

First, a couple words of caution. It is best to choose multiple items and to scramble the items on the list; that way students don't all race to the same item at the same time, and it reduces competition and noise levels in those areas of the library. It's best not to make this a competition, because students should be allowed to explore the library at their own pace and sometimes students might hide items to prevent others from finishing first. Finally, to make sure this activity is directly relevant to the project students are undertaking, we recommend that the list includes two items:

1. Find a PRINT source (something physical—book, newspaper, journal, etc.) that is relevant to the topic of your project and write a citation for it in proper APA format.
2. Check out a BOOK that contains relevant information for your topic. Show the book to your instructor before you leave.

What to do before class
It's best that students have a hardcopy of the list, so they can take notes as they go and don't have to keep checking their computer or phone. We always print them and hand them out after the short library tour (mentioned in the next section). Also, before the activity, ensure all the items on the list are in fact available at the library and haven't been checked out.

What to do during class
Begin the activity with a quick tour of the library and be sure to highlight some of the areas that students will need to accomplish the scavenger hunt. Answer any questions about the resources as you go, and then hand out the list. This activity can be done in teams or individually. While students scramble about, find a computer (or central location) where students can find you to ask questions or seek assistance.

What to do after the activity
Spot-check the assignment, but pay special attention to the citation students provide. Use this opportunity to correct any inconsistencies in their APA format.

Suggested Resources
The following is a list used for a recent scavenger hunt activity (adjustments will need to be made to match the holdings of your library):

Find the following in the library (when done, upload your answers to the appropriate dropbox on D2L):

1. The Game "Angry Animals" (or "Angry Animals 2") (hint: it's near the puppets). Which animals appear on the cover of this game? Do they look angry?
2. The moveable stacks (they're over in the back corner, by the periodicals on the first floor). Move one. Describe how it works/your process.
3. The book *Hitler's Pope*. What's the first word on page 159?
4. Describe a piece of art on the third floor. What does it look like? Where is it found? What's the title (if there is one)? Who's the author (if there is one listed)?
5. A pencil sharpener. Describe its location.
6. A government document. Describe its location. What's in the document?
7. Locate Louise Erdrich's book *Shadow Tag* in the Minnesota Studies area (hint, it's on the second floor). Who is the publisher and when was the book first published?

8. Find a PRINT source (something physical—book, newspaper, journal, etc.) that is relevant to the topic of your next project (the informative/local story) and write a citation for it in proper APA format.
9. Check out a BOOK that contains relevant information for your topic. Show the book to your instructor before you leave.

PLUG-IN ACTIVITY 8: PRACTICING RESEARCH SKILLS: APA LIBRARY RESEARCH

Objective

To engage students in an exploration and understanding of using online library databases for research

Approximate Time Required: varies; could be assigned as a homework assignment

Materials Needed
- APA library research activity worksheet (see below)
- APA style guidebook for each student

Rationale

Students often confuse online research with surfing the internet. Oftentimes, they are simply unaware of the wealth of information that the library databases provide. Sometimes they are aware of the databases, but they are unfamiliar with how to use the databases and therefore shy away from them.

This is a good activity to use after introducing the "Evaluating Websites for Source Material" activity. Students should have a base understanding of how websites are different from the articles that databases provide access to.

What to do before class
- Make copies of the worksheet or make it available via the learning management system
- Familiarize yourself with the databases you will be directing the students to use

What to do during class

Provide a brief mini-lecture on the pros of using an online database. Be sure to include the databases' core strengths in terms of research. Databases provide stronger credibility of sources accessed, better search tools and filters, and deliver higher level of content.

Walk the students through a search using the database of your choice. Heidi likes to encourage her students to use the internet for keywords and then move into an academic database to find sources for inclusion in the writing project. EBSCOhost, ProQuest, Lexis Nexis, or Academic Search Premiere are good choices with broad appeal for most composition classrooms. Show the students how to use the search tools for the database. Indicate where to find the necessary information for documenting the source in the annotated bibliography.

After an illustrative search has been completed, have the students open the worksheet and locate sources relevant to their individual projects. It is appropriate to walk around and engage with the students as they will likely find this to be a difficult process. Students will quickly learn that database search terms require more precision than a simple internet search. If the students are struggling with the search terms, it is helpful to walk them through a brainstorming activity to help define and narrow their terms.

What to do after the activity
First, celebrate the interesting information the students located in their searches. This offers them a chance to own their search results and to feel some pride at successfully navigating an academic database.

Secondly, engage the students in a discussion on why these specific databases provide stronger source material for an academic writing project. Encourage the students to transfer the sources they've located during this activity to their formal annotated bibliographies for submission in the formal MGRP.

APA Library Research Activity worksheet
Name: Topic:

Using the keywords you brainstormed for today, find **THREE** sources for your assigned essay using the college's library databases. You can either use several different databases or you can work within a specific database.

My thesis statement is:

Source #1:
Database Used to locate source:

APA References Citation:
Why is this a good source? Is there a specific place in your project where information from this source will be especially useful?

Source #2:
Database Used to locate source:

APA References Citation:
Why is this a good source? Is there a specific place in your project where information from this source will be especially useful?

Source #3:
Database Used to locate source:

APA References Citation:
Why is this a good source? Is there a specific place in your project where information from this source will be especially useful?

PLUG-IN ACTIVITY 9: SUMMARIZING USING STORIES

Objective

To encourage students to think critically about sources and to be able to successfully summarize them. To improve their listening skills, their critical thinking, their abilities with summary, and, in the process, reveal a personal narrative that helps to humanize the instructor.

Approximate Time Required: 30 minutes

Materials Needed
None

Rationale
Summary is one of the very basic tools that students need in their inventory as a writer, which is closely related to their ability to take notes from their source material. Telling a story and asking them to take notes and then summarize it is an easy way to strengthen both skills.

What to do before class
Prepare a personal narrative that you are willing to share with the class. It should be one that you've told a few times before and are very familiar with. This activity works best if you can tell the story and not read the story.

What to do during class
Let the class know you're going to tell a story and that their task is to write a summary of the story when you are finished telling it. Before beginning the story, review the core functions of summary (restating the material in your own words, condensing the original, finding the main point of the passage). Now tell the story. Be sure to give extraneous information and explore tangents; this forces students to evaluate what elements are essential to the story and which are not. Frequently, when Michael tells his story, he includes a visual related to his story. The visual can serve as a distraction from the story that's being told, further encouraging the students to take stronger notes to remain focused on the main point of the story.

When the story is done, ask students to summarize it in 250 words. Solicit volunteers to share their written summaries. It helps to have three or four volunteers, because it will reveal how different students found importance in different elements of the story.

Finally, have students summarize their summaries into one or two sentences (no more than fifty words). Again, solicit examples. The students find this to be extremely challenging, but it serves an important purpose in focusing on the main idea and not the details supporting the main idea. A discussion should follow on how detailed the summary needs to be in general. The teachable insight here is that the length of summary will depend on the purpose of the writer including it in their text. This again is a difficult concept for students to grasp, but using the two summaries, you can discuss where the longer summary would be relevant and where the briefer summary would be more appropriate.

What to do after the activity
Students typically are surprised that there is so much variety in the summaries the class creates. This is a good opportunity to address how even objective genres like summary are subject to interpretation by the writer. Ask how they arrived at what the thesis of their account was and discuss other possibilities. It often helps to write the most important elements of the story on the board and then showcase the variety of interpretations. In revealing that summary is perhaps more subjective than they originally thought, it helps to emphasize the importance of asking critical questions as they read (or listen) to better understand the argument that is being made.

Suggested Resources
MacBride, M. (2017). Breaking the ice: The teacher as "story." In Fulton, A., Field, C., & MacBride M. (Eds.), *Tell me a story: Using narratives to break down barriers in composition courses.* Lanham, MD: Rowman & Littlefield.

Chapter 5

Assessment and Evaluation

As with implementing any new class design, determining how to assess and evaluate the work is of utmost concern. When it comes to allowing students more freedom with topic, genre, and form, it can become even more problematic than usual. Are you to construct a rubric for each possible genre a student might choose to write in? How does a painting or drawing compare to something that is written? How does a poem compare to a three-page historical biographical piece? These are some of the challenges that come with integrating a creative approach to the classroom.

One method would be to create individual rubrics for each of the genres that students could choose from. In order to do this, it would mean one of two things: either, limiting the genres that students could choose from or creating rubrics as new genres arise during class. The former is the easier of the two approaches, but the latter is also feasible. Several of the educators that have taught using the MGRP involve their students in the process of determining how to evaluate the work. Tom Romano, Sirpa Grierson, Margaret Moulton, and Melinda Putz all speak of the importance of including students in the evaluation process and often the construction of the rubric for grading.

If it is a "best practice" to include students in the formation of rubrics, then it would seem possible to construct rubrics as the need arises with the assistance of the student. However, depending on the class size and number of genres, this could quickly become more cumbersome than the payoffs would justify. Additionally, students tend to want to know how their work is being assessed before they write it so that they are, at least, meeting the basic criteria.

The method that seems to be preferred in the research is that of holistic evaluation—essentially making the assessment of the MGRP a creative twist on the popular portfolio teaching method. But the question still remains: How does one evaluate a portfolio that might consist of art, collage, creative writing, research epistolary writing, journalistic writing, among others? What are the core elements that should appear on a rubric? Camille Allen, Grierson, Romano, and Nancy Mack offer several examples of holistic rubrics to use. Among their suggestions and those from other articles addressing evaluation of the MGRP, there are several categories of which scholars agree.

The MGRP literature gushes about the benefits of integrating a MGRP into a course (citing increased student motivation/engagement, instructor excitement/enthusiasm about the projects, increased knowledge transfer, among others), but none of the sources dedicate many words to assessment and evaluation. It is Michael and Heidi's hope, in this chapter, to remedy that in three ways:

1. By compiling a review of literature about assessment/evaluation,
2. Offering two concrete approaches that we use to assess the MGRP in our classes, and
3. Pointing to other possible approaches.

The authors believe it is essential that each instructor finds a method that works best for him or her; therefore, we encourage you to review our process and then adapt it to what works best in your individual classrooms.

SOME BACKGROUND

It might come as somewhat of a surprise that research indicates the element most highly regarded on rubrics is student adherence to the initial prompt and requirements of the assignment. Instructors in the scholarship who have implemented the MGRP actually have quite rigid guidelines for their students to work within. Typically, this results in the element of "adherence to the prompt" accounting for 25 to 40 percent of the MGRP grade, and "unity," "structure," or "organization" accounting for 20 to 40 percent of the student's MGRP grade. Creativity, while an important component of the project, accounts for a smaller proportion of the overall assessment.

For example, students might be allowed the freedom of topic and genres, but they are required to write in a predetermined number of genres established by the instructor. This prevents students from avoiding academic writing entirely by relying on art or creative writing to compose their project. It also allows the instructor to ensure that the core course objectives are being met through the MGRP assignment.

Additionally, critics of the MGRP assume that because the MGRP involves an element of creativity, the instructors who adopt the assignment allow the students to do whatever they want. Michael frequently encounters faculty members who are dubious of the MGRP approach and assume it doesn't require the rigor of a "traditional" research paper. However, he assures them that it is considerably more difficult to weave together disparate genres of writing than it is to construct a lengthy (often padded) research project.

Though the MGRP might offer an opportunity for creativity, it is overwhelmingly intellectual creativity; furthermore, for the MGRP to work, it must have an overriding thesis, just as the beloved "traditional" research paper. David LeNoir (2002) addresses this in his article "The Multigenre Warning Label":

> In simple terms, a multigenre work without unity is not a multigenre paper... simply assembling [poetry, essays, articles, letter, paintings, etc.] in the same document serves no purpose. The point of a multigenre paper is to convey a unified message through means that reflect the richness of the experience, so this unity must be reflected not only in the content of the individual elements, but also by how they work together. (p. 100)

While on the surface, the MGRP appears to allow substantial freedom, students still must find this thread that will unify the items together and truly make it a project and not, as LeNoir (2002) suggests, "an anthology" (p. 100). Teaching students to find this thread forces them to understand the concept of synthesis, which is a key element of any research project.

Finally, it's valuable to note here that a MGRP would not be a research project without, well, *research*. As such, it should come as no surprise that research is also highly regarded as a core element of any rubric designed for the MGRP course. The range for this category is 30 to 50 percent of the project grade. While the scholarship agrees that research is an essential aspect of the assignment, there are concerns about respecting the integrity of the art.

Basically, scholars maintain is it important not to clutter the genres with citations so it can most resemble the "real" genre it is mirroring. However, in order to require students to utilize their research, and for instructors to be able to evaluate how and where students are using their sources, it is necessary for some kind of documentation to occur (besides the matter of trying to teach students to avoid plagiarism and learn proper citation for their sources).

The solution for Romano, and hence others since (Allen, Bowen, Moulton, Putz), is to require annotated bibliographies and extensive endnotes. While endnotes might be seen as intruding upon the "art," they are necessary to point to the specific piece of information in the text, to allow students to indicate where the information is from, and to explain how each source assisted them.

In the case of a piece of art, no numbers need to be explicitly located on the drawing, but an explication of the work needs to accompany it—explaining why the creative work was created this way, why these colors, why this pose, why this composition. The annotated bibliography is also an essential method of tracking student research. In addition to the usual summary of the sources, annotations should also include explanations of how these sources were helpful in generally developing each MGRP and specifically where and how each source is used.

Reflection is the element of the rubrics that varied the most, sometimes as high as 50 percent and others as low as 10 percent. It should be noted that, like any other teaching approach, these numbers fluctuated widely with each new attempt (sometimes Romano's rubric accounted for 50 percent, others as little as 20 percent). In either case, the concept of reflection is an essential component to this assignment.

Kathleen Blake Yancey (2001) defines reflection as "a dialectical process by which we develop and achieve, first, specific goals for learning; second, strategies for reaching those goals; and third, means of determining whether or not we have met those goals or other goals" (p. 6). Putz (2006) picks up on a few of Yancey's points asserting that "often if [students] take time to do [reflection], they not only realize where their projects are deficient but also what they've learned and how much they've grown" (p. 130). Reflection can also come in the form of student journals (Allen, 2001; Moulton, 1999; Romano, 2000), learning logs (particularly in Romano, 2000), and post-write exercises after the completion of the MGRP (Romano, 2000; Murray, Shea, & Shea, 2004).

With significant reflection in mind, the potential of MGRP for composition courses becomes more apparent. While reflection is beginning to be recognized as an essential element of any learning process, it is perhaps even more so with the MGRP because of its potential to be thought of as pieces rather than a whole.

ASSESSMENT IN THE COLLEGE/UNIVERSITY CLASSROOM

While these suggestions for evaluation of MGRPs come from examples of instructors using this approach in secondary education, the transition to a "university" setting is quite simple because the university values the same elements listed above. Reflection, as addressed in the previous paragraph, is fast becoming a requirement of writing courses and having students engage in reflective writing is now seen as a "best practice."

Cohesion, structure, organization, and unity are all key elements of good writing; there must be something that ties the paragraphs together, and the MGRP is simply an extension of that. Documentation, citation, and annotation are all essential components of any writing that involves research and secondary sources.

Following instructions and adhering to the writing prompt is also a necessity for any writing class (following instructions is essential for any course and nearly everything down to assembly of pre-packaged furniture and children's toys). All that remains is to tweak the assignment to fit the requirements of the university setting, which really is no different than adjusting a teaching approach to accommodate students of greater ability.

Tweaking the assignment can be as simple as reducing the number of, or restricting the type of, genres required. Requiring students to write their MGRP using three to five genres is reasonable. This should allow them plenty of time to fully explore the genres of their choice and produce a piece that is carefully thought out. If there is a concern about students not doing enough actual writing, then the genres can be further restricted or a minimum requirement of words can be established.

In terms of the evaluation of such a project, the guidelines set forth by the research suggest that it should consist of the four components addressed earlier: research/documentation, unity/cohesion/structure/organization, reflection, and following prompt/assignment requirements. One possible breakdown of percentages could be: 30 percent for research/documentation, 30 percent for following prompt/assignment requirements, 20 percent for organization/structure, and 20 percent for reflection. However, there is one other important element to address that has not been mentioned thus far—process.

All of the above assessment suggestions address the actual product and not the process the student took to achieve the product (though, it could be argued the reflection activities should include indications of process). As such, and this is something the MGRP instructors agree on, assessment must occur along the way. In order for the MGRP to be successful, students must receive guidance throughout the course of the project. This should involve checkpoints (or "mileposts," as Richison, Hernandez, and Carter (2002) refer to them) along the way, where students' research is evaluated, their topics discussed, guidance offered, and their ideas are shared with fellow students. Just as with most portfolio projects, students need deadlines or checkpoints to help them keep pace and to make sure they are on the right track.

As a result, the process students take toward achieving completion of their MGRP could account for a large percentage of the final grade. Per the aforementioned research, in most cases, process consists of 40–50 percent of the student's final grade for the unit; the portfolio consists of the remaining percentage. Obviously, these numbers can be adjusted to suit different settings and curriculums, but it is important that students receive some evaluation before their MGRP is due (both for their sanity and the instructor's as well). This can be in the form of "learning logs" (Moulton, 1999, p. 530; Romano, 1995, p. 144), "student response journals" (Allen, 2001, p. 113), a presentation of findings thus far (Allen, 2001, p. 122; Grierson, 1999, p. 54; Putz, 2006, p. 133), "peer evaluations" (Putz, 2006, p. 133), periodic reviews of the student's annotated bibliography, or any combination of the above.

Though process certainly is a vital piece of the project, Heidi and Michael believe that the substantial weight of the grade should be on the product produced and not the method by which the student took to complete it. Instead, "process" points should be accumulated through in-class activities, and the MGRP would be graded separate from any "process activities." In that way, the MGRP is graded as any other essay assignment would be.

THE PORTFOLIO APPROACH

Because the MGRP is a multi-part project that develops over a protracted period of time, and, because many schools have adopted some version of a portfolio program, the portfolio approach to assessment is attractive. There is, in fact, a lot of overlap in the theories governing both the portfolio and the MGRP. For instance, Kathy McClelland's (1991) comments about portfolios, in her essay "Portfolios: Solution to a Problem," could just as easily come from any of the literature about MGRPs: "Time allows the students to develop a sense of authority over their texts" (as cited in Belanoff & Dickson, 1991, p. 171).

By allowing students to become "quasi-experts" about a topic (whether that topic is their own writing, as in the case of portfolios, or a topic of their choosing in the case of the MGRP), they then develop ownership (authority) over their texts and take extra care in how they write, why they make the rhetorical decisions they do, and how they select the texts to be included. These decisions, and the awareness that comes from them, are essential to developing critical writers.

Indeed, it is Yancey's (2001) comments about portfolios that resonate most soundly with regard to MGRPs: "Portfolios . . . are unified as a construct. Created by the three principal activities of collection, selection, and reflection" (p. 16). While the MGRP is indeed a "collection" of student writing, and "selection" and "reflection" are certainly essential to creating a cohesive MGRP and reinforcing learning, there is an important difference between the two approaches.

The portfolio is an opportunity for the student to select his or her writing that is best representative of growth over the course of the semester; by contrast, the MGRP forces the student to continually make selections throughout the project that best serve the eventual final "product." Certainly, during a period of revision, a student may choose to discard an earlier installment of the MGRP, or to rewrite it entirely, but the true boon of the MGRP is that, in constructing a cohesive project (rather than simply a collection of work done over the course of a semester), the student is pushed to continually reflect, select, and collect the genres that best serve his or her MGRP.

Ultimately, there are things that can be borrowed from portfolio assessment and applied to assessing the MGRP. Ricky Lam (2013) suggests that portfolios "productively foster SRL (self-regulated learning)" (p. 699) because they are "a collection of students' works-in-progress and final drafts that they have created over time" (p. 702). Ane Qvortrup and Tina Bering Keiding (2015) argue that portfolios, "by scaffolding both reflection and reflexivity, produce particular conditions for the stimulation and observation of learning" (p. 407).

Brian Huot (2002), in *(Re)articulating Writing Assessment for Teaching and Learning*, writes that "portfolios undermine the current assumption that is possible to ascertain a student's ability to write from one piece of writing, or that writing or a writer's development can be inferred incrementally through the evaluation of individual products or an aggregate of individual evaluations" (p. 72). Huot (2002) goes on to echo Yancey's comments about the importance of selection and reflection: "Reflection and writing about writing focus not only on the product of writing but on the process as well, demonstrating what the student writer knows about the product and process of writing within her own experience as a writer" (p. 72).

It is important to assess student writing, but perhaps even more important to gain insight into a student's awareness about the decisions he or she is making. Huot (2002), and other proponents of the portfolio approach, suggest "ungraded but responded-to writing" (p. 73) that builds up to the final assessment of the portfolio. In that way, students gain constructive feedback from their instructors while not being burdened with the pressure of an actual grade. While this is well intentioned, it places too great a weight on the portfolio grade for first-year composition students. Rather, as stated earlier, we suggest "checkpoint" or "milestone" assessments on the individual pieces of the MGRP. In that way, students receive constructive feedback and a better sense of where they stand with regard to grades.

Grades are a simple reality of the university. They can be a powerful motivating force, and they can absolutely discourage those that try and fail. Ultimately, as Timothy Quinn (2013) claims, there are three primary goals of grading systems: to "generate data with which decisions can be made about future practice, to motivate students, and to provide them with feedback" (p. 24). To prevent discouragement, Quinn (2013) goes on to suggest the use of "common rubrics" that are generated through collaboration with other writing instructors.

The hope is to find "universal" criteria for evaluation. While such consensus on criteria may seem difficult to assemble, Bob Broad's (2003) *What We Really Value: Beyond Rubrics in Teaching and Assessing Writing* summarizes the work of early writing assessment groups that did just that: "Succinctly, their fifty-five types of comments were boiled down to: idea, style, organization, paragraphing, sentence structure, mechanics, and verbal facility" (p. 6).

And, paraphrasing Lester Faigley, Broad (2003) simplifies the criteria one step further, to: ideas, form, flavor, mechanics, wording (p. 6).

Though these may be common criteria that some (or even most) instructors can relate to, Marie C. Paretti and Katrina M. Powell (2009) remind: "Even while assessment methods such as holistic scoring and portfolio assessment can be used across contexts, the standards used to evaluate writing must always be developed locally and take into consideration the course, the discipline, and the faculty expectations that guided the writing" (p. 5). Furthermore, best practices require that "assessment should use multiple measures . . . and analyze multiple artifacts of student writing" (p. 30). These are elements that are automatically included in a MGRP by the very virtue of the assignment.

Patricia Lynne (2004), in *Coming to Terms: A Theory of Writing Assessment*, reminds us that, "objectivity has been the primary driving force behind contemporary assessment" (p. 40) and it "grew out of a desire in part for more equitable and meaningful assessment, ideals few educators would reject today" (p. 43). Despite all of the exciting opportunities that the MGRP offers, remaining objective during assessment is one of the largest obstacles (and the same can be said for portfolios).

The more familiar an instructor is with a student's work, and the more an instructor sees the same work in various stages (whether throughout the course of a semester that builds to a portfolio or in drafts building to a MGRP), the more likely the instructor is to be swayed by process and a personal connection to the student and his or her work. It is with this idea in mind that Heidi and Michael strongly encourage graded components of the MGRP throughout the course of the semester and not simply a graded "portfolio" at the end of the term.

MICHAEL'S APPROACH

Michael uses the same rubric for individual assignments and the end of the semester finished MGRP; there are several reasons for this. First, using the same grade sheet ensures that students are familiar with the expectations and that they are being held to the same standards as the class objectives. Second, it alleviates the necessity to create grade sheets on the fly. By condensing the core criteria of the assignment into four elements, it simplifies the grading process and allows for flexibility with interpreting those criteria for each project, or component of the project. Finally, it challenges students to creatively meet each of the expectations regardless of the genre a student chooses.

In order to ensure familiarity, students grade former student projects using the rubric. This activity encourages students to become familiar with the requirements of the assignments inside and out. It ensures a fuller understanding of the criteria by which the assignment (that they themselves are in fact in the process of creating) is graded. Further, it exposes students to student work revealing potential projects, ideas, use of genres, and the very fact that others have completed this activity before them and succeeded.

Before students grade the activities, they first read and reflect on the grade sheet. Michael asks them what each of the criteria mean to them, how they believe somebody could meet those expectations, and what questions they have for understanding these expectations. This discussion typically offers an opportunity to see how well the students are able to understand the grading sheet. After students have graded projects, Michael conducts a norming session where grades and comments are shared and discussed. Throughout the course of the discussion, students have to defend their evaluation of the projects by using the grade sheet to structure their argument.

Additionally, students want to know the score that was actually given to the projects and are often surprised when, typically, students have graded their peers more harshly than their instructor had. While individuals may have scored a particular project higher or lower than Michael, the class average usually ends up being very close to the score assessment of the assignment. This reinforces the idea that while there is some level of objectivity to the instructor's evaluation of student work, the grade is not based solely on the instructor's opinion.

Michael has also found it beneficial to create his own MGRP to share with his class. This allows him to anticipate pitfalls and struggles that students might encounter. Additionally, he has found that students thoroughly enjoy the opportunity to critique their instructor's writing. In doing so, students realize that their instructor is a writer also, and that writing is hard work even for those more proficient at it. Each of these discussions is an opportunity to explore aspects of writing that students are not typically privy to.

In order for students to be able to grade and evaluate assignments, they first must understand the criteria for assessment. Michael's rubric (see page 125 in the "Appendix L") has four basic criteria: quality and use of research; organization, development, structure; grammar and mechanics; and creativity.

At first glance, it might be difficult to see how a category like "quality and use of research" may be relevant to a poem, short story, or a more creative component. However, because students know that this is a criterion by which their work will be evaluated, it needs to be incorporated and challenges them to think of creative ways to do just that. In the past, students have included an author's note or critical introduction, utilized footnotes and endnotes, and included an annotated bibliography. The onus is not on the instructor but on the student to determine the most appropriate way to incorporate that element into his or her project. By leaving it open to interpretation and possibility, students frequently surprise their instructor with their innovation.

Similarly, an ambiguous criterion such as "creativity" is also met in unexpected ways. In previous grade sheets, Michael did not have a category for creativity, but he quickly realized it was disingenuous not to include it simply because it was always subconsciously a criterion he considered. However, in a formal first-year composition course, creativity cannot account for a sizable percentage of the grade. It could, however, account for the difference between a "B" and an "A." Including "creativity" on the grade sheet is simply an attempt to be as transparent to students about what matters in the course of evaluation.

Furthermore, as discussed in the first chapter, the emphasis for creativity in this project is intellectual. This means pushing students to think of creative topics to begin with, but also to choose a unique angle to write from. It means finding gaps in the historical record and making connections where ones are not immediately obvious. Rather than rewarding a clever title or a poem with a gold star for creativity, Heidi and Michael challenge their students to find a unique lens to look through and to actually say something "new."

When Michael grades student work, he leaves a combination of specific and holistic feedback. For each criterion, he leaves a comment that speaks generally about how the student writing met that objective, and he leaves specific examples from the student work on the grade sheet. He prefers this method to using electronic in-text comments or writing on student work for a couple of reasons. First, he remembers being a student and being overwhelmed by the red marks all over his work and doesn't want to subject his students to that. Second, by choosing specific moments to highlight as examples of trends throughout the student's work, it forces students to go back through their work and fix similar errors, thus reinforcing the behavior or role in the student's mind.

A former instructor once told Michael that simply circling all of the homonym confusion in an essay simply provides a crutch to the student and allows him or her to continue to limp along. Additionally, that same instructor said, ten comma splices aren't ten errors, they are simply one error repeated ten times—get to the root of the problem and pull that weed. Finally, it also forces Michael to think critically about what matters most in the evaluation of the student's work.

HEIDI'S APPROACH

As Michael points out, students benefit from milestones within the project with assessment and feedback along the way. This is true not only for the semester-long implementation of the MGRP but also for the self-contained unit that Heidi teaches. The MGRP is a huge project that needs feedback along the way to help the students fully satisfy the objectives of the assignment.

When Heidi assesses the final MGRPs, a clearly defined rubric best matches her temperament for fairness in grading the final project. She has found that without a clearly stated rubric, her assessment is susceptible to being too lenient. She finds that she can become entangled in the effort that went into the final project to justify a higher grade. It's easy to become enamored with the students' process and dedication to their projects.

However, because the MGRP is a requirement for credit in a college-level writing course, assessing merely on effort is incongruous with the purpose of the project, which is for the students to demonstrate mastery of writing skills as stated in the core learning objectives. While it is difficult to assign a poor grade to a student who has obviously taken tremendous effort with the project but who has failed to meet the goals of the assignment (unity, research, use of genre, creativity), a strong rubric helps communicate the rationale behind the assigned grade.

It stands to reason, then, that there is great value in providing substantial feedback throughout the duration of the project to help facilitate adherence to the expectations of the assignment and ultimately, to the rubric. As Heidi notes in chapter 2, as she outlines the rollout of the assignment, there are several places built into the unit where pointed feedback encourages students to stay on track with the objectives of the assignment. If the instructor is diligent in providing feedback at the various checkpoints offered in chapter 2, the expectation is that all student projects will meet the basic requirements of the final submission of the MGRP.

The rubric Heidi has created (see page 127 in the appendix) for the assessment of the MGRP self-contained unit favors a balance of focus and organization (25 percent), content (25 percent), use of sources (25 percent), grammar, syntax, mechanics, formatting (15 percent), and creativity (10 percent).

To begin, a clear assignment sheet helps the students focus their projects from the beginning. Be clear in expectations for overall unity, use of research (and quality), creativity, and adherence to genre forms for each piece of writing. Heidi finds it useful to emphasize several times throughout the unit that all of these components are necessary to the final project. She stresses that the project is ultimately an academic research project that has to have singular focus with strong unity. Simply submitting an anthology of genres with no clear purpose will not meet expectations.

To achieve a strong assessment in focus and organization, the project must have a unified focus where all the pieces are ordered in a logical progression, each piece building on the preceding piece. The variety of genres must have some relationship to each other to build a unifying thread within the project. For example, if a student wants to use an obituary, a business letter, a job posting, and a newspaper article, what is the unifying factor that ties them all together? How does each piece build off the other to provide deeper content for the reader?

To illustrate: The student's MGRP subject might be to explore the impact that Jim Valvano, a well-respected ESPN broadcaster, had on the industry. The student could begin his project with the obituary of Valvano, followed by a business letter within ESPN indicating the need to replace Valvano and the requirements the new candidate would need to fill Valvano's vacancy, an official posting of the job vacancy (highlighting the things Valvano did in the position), and finally a newspaper article lauding Valvano's career while introducing his replacement. Everything in the student's project is geared toward helping the reader better understand why Jim Valvano was so well respected in his field.

One of the main objectives of the MGRP is for the project to provide interesting and impactful content for the reader. Heidi is constantly checking in on the students' research to ensure that they are taking their research/content to a level that's appropriate for an academic audience. She reminds them that the MGRP is teaching them to research *new* things instead of simply finding research that supports what they already know about their subjects.

This is generally one of those "light bulb" moments for the students. Initially, many of them choose subjects that they already know a lot about because they think it will make the project simpler to compile. Once they understand that the purpose of the project is as much for the student to learn more about the research topic as it is for the reader, their attitude about it tends to shift. Heidi has had more than one student state on the final self-reflection something to the effect of, "I thought I knew everything there was to know about my topic! I learned so much doing this project."

Being able to locate, evaluate, and integrate source material is a core course objective for most first-year composition courses. For that reason, it carries a heavy percentage of the rubric for the final assessment. Again, Heidi checks in with the students frequently to see what sources they are using for their projects. This helps the students learn by process what quality sources look like. In Heidi's experience, the students' understanding of appropriate sources increases tremendously as the project progresses.

These check-ins are valuable for the assessment component in the rubric that refers to the use of quality sources. If the instructor waits to address the use of sources until the final project is submitted, the quality of sources is typically disappointing (as has been the case with most traditional research paper projects Heidi has assigned in the past). Furthermore, if the conversation about quality sources occurs after the final project is assessed, an opportunity for the student to learn in process is lost.

Grammar, syntax, mechanics, and formatting carry a slightly less significant percentage in the final rubric. This is because a college-level writing project must be able to demonstrate mastery of the basic rules of writing, but by this point in the semester, the students should have learned to polish their writing to eliminate these errors. Heidi encourages her students to be diligent in their proofing of the final projects prior to submission because mechanical errors can be distracting to the reader. More importantly, mechanical errors can undermine their credibility as academic researchers and writers.

Finally, while creativity is difficult to measure, it's an important component of the assessment of this project. What is meant by creativity is simply this:

- *Intellectual creativity*: Has the student shown a capacity to make connections between sources and genres that go beyond the obvious? Did they "see" something new and incorporate that into the final project?
- *Aesthetic creativity*: Does the project look nice? Has the student taken initiative to create a cover that matches the content of the project? It's not about being artistic; it's about being able to create a format/layout in the project that is pleasing to the eye in some regard.

The use of rubrics for formal assessment has both its weaknesses and strengths. Some instructors are opposed to its use due to the rigidity it imposes on assessment. However, when it comes to the assessment of the MGRP in a college composition classroom, it can be a valuable tool in keeping the assessment of the finished project focused on the core objectives that the project is intended to meet. It eliminates some of the innate subjectivity the instructor brings to the project. It also helps justify the grade easily to the student, who has invested much time and energy in the project and might be prone to taking the grade personally.

REFERENCES

Allen, C. A. (2001). *Multigenre research paper: Voice, passion, and discovery in grades 4–6*. Portsmouth, NH: Heinemann.

Broad, B. (2003). *What we really value: Beyond pubrics in teaching and assessing writing*. Logan, UT: Utah State University Press.

Grierson, S. T. (1999, September). Circling through text: Teaching research through multigenre writing. *The English Journal, 89*(1), 51–55.

Huot, B. (2002). *(Re)articulating writing assessment for teaching and learning*. Logan, UT: Utah State University Press.

Lam, R. (2013, November). Promoting Self-Regulated Learning Through Portfolio Assessment: Testimony and Recommendations. *Assessment & Evaluation in Higher Education, 39*(6), 699–714. doi: 10.1080/02602938.2013.862211

LeNoir, W. D. (2002, November). The multigenre warning label. *The English Journal, 92*(2), 99–101.

Lynne, P. (2004). *Coming to terms: A theory of writing assessment*. Logan, UT: Utah State University Press.

Mack, N. (2002, November). The ins, outs, and in-betweens of multigenre writing. *English Journal 92*(2), 91–98.

Mack, N. (2006). Ethical representation of working-class lives: Multiple genres, voices, and identities. *Pedagogy, 6*(1), 53–78.

Mack, N. (2013). Multigenre report writing: Teaching handouts. *Dr. Nancy Mack.* Retrieved from http://www.wright.edu/~nancy.mack/mghandouts.htm.

Mack, N. (2015). *Engaging writers with multigenre research projects: A teacher's guide.* New York: Teachers College Press.

McClelland, K. (1991). Portfolios: Solution to a problem. In P. Belanoff & M. Dickson (Eds.), *Portfolios: Process and product* (pp. 165–173). Portsmouth, NH: Heinemann.

Moulton, M. R. (1999, April). The multigenre paper: Increasing interest, motivation, and functionality in research. *Journal of Adolescent & Adult Literacy, 42*(7), 528–539.

Murray, R., Shea, M., & Shea, B. (2004, Fall). Avoiding the one-size-fits-all curriculum: Textsets, inquiry, and differentiating instruction. *Childhood Education, 81*(1), 33–35.

Paretti, M. C., & Powell, K. M. (2009). *Assessment of writing* (Vol. 4). Tallahassee, FL: Association for Institutional Research.

Putz, M. (2006). *A teacher's guide to the multigenre research project.* Portsmouth, NH: Heinemann.

Quinn, T. (2013). *On grades and grading.* Lanham, MD: Rowman & Littlefield.

Qvortrup, A., & Keiding, T. B. (2015). Portfolio assessment: Production and reduction of complexity. *Assessment & Evaluation in Higher Education, 40*(3), 407–419.

Richison, J., Hernandez, A. C., & Carter, M. (2002, November). Blending multiple genres in theme baskets. *English Journal, 92*(2), 76–81.

Romano, T. (1987). Making the grade in evaluation: Keep students writing. *Clearing the Way: Working with teenage writers* (pp. 107–129). Portsmouth, NH: Heinemann.

Romano, T. (1995). *Writing with passion: Life stories, multiple genres.* Portsmouth, NH: Boynton & Cook.

Romano, T. (2000). *Blending genre, altering style.* Portsmouth, NH: Heinemann.

Romano, T. (2002). Teaching writing through multigenre papers. In R. Tremmel and W. Broz (Eds.), *Teaching Writing Teachers of High School and First Year Composition* (pp. 52–65). Portsmouth, NH: Boynton/Cook Pub.

Romano, T. (2004, March 8). The multigenre paper. *Teachers College of Columbia University.* Retrieved from http://www.tc.columbia.edu/centers/mssc/Downloads/The%20Multigenre%20Paper.doc.

Romano, T. (2013). *Fearless writing: Multigenre to motivate and inspire.* Portsmouth, NH: Heinemann.

Yancey, K B. (2001). Digitized student portfolios. In B. Cambridge (Ed.), *Electronic portfolios: Emerging practices in student, faculty, and institutional learning* (pp. 15–30). Washington, DC: American Association for Higher Education.

Appendix A

Assignment Sheet for MGRP Self-Contained Unit

Length: Minimum total word count of 2,500

Due dates: 50% completion: {date}
　　　　　　　Draft complete: {date}
　　　　　　　Final project due: {date}

Source Requirement:

** Annotated Bibliography with 15 entries
** Minimum of 7 sources cited within the MRP

INTRODUCTION

A multigenre research project is simply a research project that is broken down into several different genres. These are often called "crots," but for the sake of clarity, we will refer to them as pieces. The goal of a MGRP is to learn to research a subject so thoroughly that you can write about it using several different genres and rhetorical choices. Although we will be practicing many different writing styles, the end goal is the same as any traditional research paper: to create a well-researched project with strong unity, new and interesting information, and well-thought out rhetorical choices.

THE ASSIGNMENT REQUIREMENTS

- You will submit a project that has an overall minimum of 2,500 words.
- Your project will have a *minimum* of five different pieces of writing. These can be from any genre you choose—your focus can be formal, fun, creative, etc. You choose your own adventure.

- You will need to employ a *minimum* of four different genres. These can be songs, poems, formal essays, memos, obituaries, news articles, etc. There is an exhaustive list of genre in the content section of the MGRP in D2L.
- Your use of each genre must show adherence of style to that particular genre; that is, if you are using a formal business letter for one of your pieces, then your business letter must adhere to the expected norms of a formal business letter. You might have to do additional research for stylistic expectations on the specifics of some genres. You can always ask me, too.
- Two of your pieces are not optional: You must submit an overview/background/summary (informative genre) and an annotated bibliography (see separate assignment sheets on both of these requirements).
- Your topic must be real. While there is ample room for creativity in this project, the goal is to research something to communicate a stronger understanding of that subject to your reader. In this manner, a creative narrative of your life will not work; a made up story will not work; research on mythical creatures would work.
- Borrowed material will be clearly marked through formal documentation (APA), the use of direct quotes or introduced summaries. References sections are included when necessary. Bibliography sections are used when more appropriate.

Deadlines and other important things:
- Project proposal is due {date}—once your subject is chosen, you will not be able to change it. You can change the focus/thesis statement, but not the subject.
- Assignment #1, overview/background/summary is due {date}. This will count as one of the pieces in the final MGRP.
- Assignment #2, a working annotated bibliography, is due {date} and with the final submission. This will count as one of the pieces in the final project.
- Assignment #3, an update on your project, is due {date}. Your project should be 50 percent complete now. This is NOT one of the pieces for the final project. *This will be separate from the final project submission.*
- In-class work days will be {dates}. We will also have in-class conferences during these two weeks.
- Complete draft of project is due {date}.
- Group presentations of project and final submission will be {date}.
- Assessed projects will be available for during finals week (time and date to be determined).

Appendix B

MGRP Topic Proposal Handout for Self-Contained Unit

Proposal for subject approval

Due date:

— I understand what the multigenre research project (MGRP) is what the assignment expectations are for me
— I do **not** understand the MGRP and would like to schedule a conference with you, the instructor, to better understand it

My two topic choices are:

Top choice:

Alternative choice:

Why do you think your top choice is a good topic choice for the MGRP?

What do you already know about this topic?

What are some things you want to learn about your topic through the research process?

Appendix B

What are some potential pieces of writing for your project (fill in the table below)?

Piece of writing (include type of genre)	What kind of information might you provide with this piece of writing?

Appendix C

Assignment Sheet for Whole Semester Adaptation

INTRODUCTION

As the name implies, this assignment will require research. That part should be straightforward. You'll have to select a topic that you can find research on and then figure out how to incorporate it into your larger project. The part that might be causing you to wonder is the "multigenre" part.

But, don't let it scare you. The "multi" part just means, well . . . multiple. More than one. More than two (since that's a couple). Three, maybe. Maybe four. However many is up to you. The "genre" part in this case means "form" or "type." So, all it means is that you'll be doing multiple types/forms of writing.

What are some of the forms that you might use? I like to leave it open-ended, but I also understand the need for some examples. So, here goes:

Biography	Obituary	Letters
Police report	Advertisement	Journal article
Greeting card	Diary/journal	To do list
Grocery list	Recipe	Memo
Online chat/IM transcript	Speech	Epitaph
Questionnaire/survey	Note to self/reminder	Interview
Song	Poem	Short story
News article	Novel (or excerpt?)	Textbook (or excerpt?)
Directions	Memoir/Autobiography	Menu
Propaganda	Flyer	Map
Leaflets	Painting	Screenplay (or excerpt?)
Religious materials	Photograph (they're worth 1,000 words, right?)	Reference materials (from a dictionary, encyclopedia, or something similar)

... and I'm sure there are others. But, that should give you some ideas.

The nitty gritty of the assignment:
- By the end of the semester, you will have produced a project that contains at least 5,000 words of your own writing
- However, the final project can (and perhaps should) include things other than your own writing: paintings, drawings, maps, photographs, and perhaps even someone else's writing (newspaper articles, poetry, song lyrics, etc.)
- You must use *at least* three different genres/types/forms in your project. These are not limited to the list above, and if you have any question . . . just ask.
- How you divide the page requirement between the five required assignments is also up to you
- I do require that there is at least one biographic or historical piece that provides an overview of your topic to your reader
- But, the genres/types/forms you choose are entirely up to you
- The **assignment #6** (annotated bibliography) is a part of this project and is really an ongoing assignment, because you will be recording your sources that you've used, how you used them, and why you used them.
- **Your topic** must be "real." By this, I mean you cannot have invented it. You must be able to find research on the topic. It can be a mythical creature like *el chupacabra*, as long as you can find documents that talk about it.
- How are these individual assignments graded? See the rubric on D2L for full details. But, basically, according to four main criteria: (1) quality and use of research; (2) organization, development, and structure; (3) grammar and mechanics; and (4) creativity.

Deadlines:
- To get the gears going, you must submit a proposal for the topic that you're considering by **the second week of the semester**. This proposal can be fairly informal. Essentially, I'm looking for about two pages. What topic are you interested in doing? Why? What do you already know about the topic? What kind of genres do you think will work best for this type of project? Why? You can certainly change your topic after that point, but it only makes more work for you. Selecting a topic is important. And, since you'll be working with this topic all semester . . . you'll want to pick something that you are interested in learning and writing about.
- By **the third week of the semester** your first installment is due. This first piece should be something that provides background or an overview of the topic or an aspect of the topic. A biography, obituary, historical document, newspaper article, or something along those lines works well.

- We will have peer review days, where you bring in your work, share it with others, receive feedback from them, and give them feedback on theirs. So, there will be deadlines for steps of the assignment along the way to make sure everyone has something ready by these days.
- Typically the class period after peer review day will be the day that I collect whichever portion of your project that you're working at that time, so I can grade it and provide feedback of my own.

Appendix D

Assignment Sheet for Assignment #1: Overview/Summary/Background

ASSIGNMENT #1: OVERVIEW/BACKGROUND/SUMMARY

Length: Aim for a minimum of 400 words

Due dates: {date}

Source Requirement: minimum of three sources (APA documentation with formal References)

You will write an overview, summary, or informative background piece for your first piece of writing in the multigenre research project (MGRP). The purpose of this piece is to familiarize your reader with your subject in a broad sense so that the reader can easily identify the meaningfulness of the accompanying pieces. The goal is to establish the focus and intent of the overall project. Remember, unity is one of the main objectives of the MGRP, so be intentional in creating a strong thesis statement that supports the overall purpose of the MGRP.

You're going to have to use multiple sources in this overview/summary/background piece. Part of the assessment on this piece will be on your ability to synthesize multiple sources of research and integrate them into your writing. This will require formal APA in-text citations as well as a formal References page.

Appendix E

Workshop for Assignment #1: MGRP Self-Contained Unit

WORKSHOP FOR ASSIGNMENT #1: OVERVIEW/ BACKGROUND/SUMMARY

Read your partners Assignment #1 Background/Summary/Overview document carefully. Then answer the following questions the best you can. If you cannot answer a question, based on your understanding of the project, please note that for the writer.

Does the essay reach the required length: (should be a minimum of 400 words)?

Does the author meet the minimum source requirement: Three sources (APA documentation with formal References)?

What is the overall purpose of the project?

Do you think the focus is appropriate for the project? Why or why not?

What are some questions that you hope the rest of the project will be able to answer?

Appendix E

Do you find the subject interesting? Why or why not?

Does the writer use formal APA documentation to cite three or more sources?

Is there a References page to match the in-text citations?

Please give the writer three suggestions for piece of writing he or she might use to develop the rest of the project. Be mindful to keep the writer's thesis statement in mind so you can help keep his or her project unified.

What have you learned from this workshop that you will apply to your own project?

Your name:

Project author:

Appendix F

Checklist for Workshop Day

Multigenre Research Project: A choose your own adventure research project

- ∈ Total word count exceeds 2,500 (total word count is: _____)
- ∈ Five pieces of writing are included (total number of pieces is: _____)
- ∈ Four different genres are represented (list each used: _____ _____ _____)
- ∈ Seven sources within the overall project are cited using (Author, date) and page number when applicable.
- ∈ Title Page includes Title, Name, Date, and Class
- ∈ Table of Contents lists all pieces by title of piece (and not by genre)
- ∈ Each piece of writing has a Bibliography with at least two sources listed in formal APA format
- ∈ Piece #1 has a formal References page with matching in-text citations

How to assemble the final project for submission:

- Copy and paste all the pieces into a new Word document (save first as Final MGRP_LastName)
- Turn non-digital files into .pdf, .jpeg, or .tif files. Insert these into separate Word documents for integration into the final document.
- Be sure the final project has all the required pieces included: Title page, table of contents, at least five pieces of writing representing at least four different genres (including a formal Annotated Bibliography).
- Once everything is in one big document, insert page numbers.
- Once page numbers have been inserted, double check the table of contents to make sure it matches up.
- Create a running header along the upper right header: "Multigenre Research Project Final: {last name}"
- Save to the folder titled "Multigenre Research Project Final"

Ask for help in inserting page numbers, page breaks, or orientation of pages in Word documents.

Appendix F

Rotate a page to landscape or portrait orientation

You can choose either portrait (vertical) or landscape (horizontal) orientation for all or part of your document.

Change the orientation of your entire document

1. Click > **Page Layout** > **Orientation**.

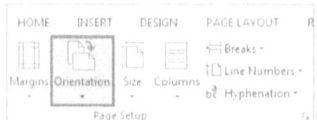

2. Click **Portrait** or **Landscape**.

Note When you change the orientation, the cover pages in the Cover Page gallery change to the orientation you've chosen.

Use different orientations in the same document

There may be times when you want certain pages or sections of your document to have a different orientation from the rest of it. Note that Word puts selected text on its own page, and the surrounding text on separate pages.

1. Select the pages or paragraphs whose orientation you want to change.
2. Click **Page Layout** > **Page Setup** Dialog Box Launcher.

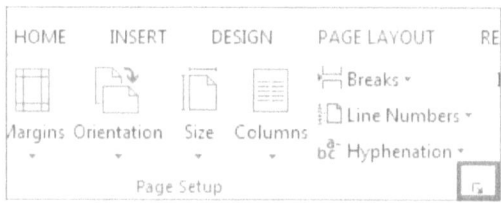

1. In the **Page Setup** box, under **Orientation**, click **Portrait** or **Landscape**.

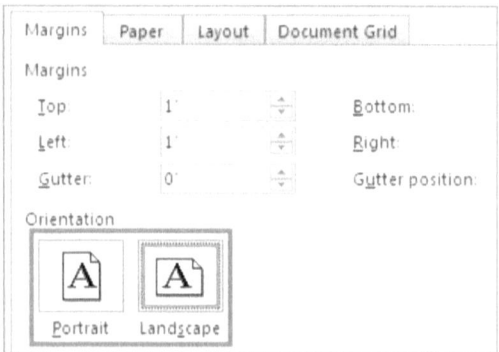

1. Click the **Apply to** box and click **Selected text**.

Appendix F 111

Note Word automatically inserts section breaks before and after the text that has the new page orientation. If your document is already divided into sections, you can click in a section (or select multiple sections), and then change the orientation for only the sections that you select. Read about how to find out where the section breaks are in your document.

Add a PDF to a document

You can insert a PDF into a Word document as an object that you can open and view. You'll be able to re-size it, but you can't edit it.

1. Click **Insert > Object**.

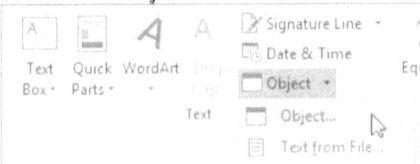

2. In the **Object** dialog box, click **Create from File** and then click **Browse**.
3. Find the PDF you want to insert, and then click **Insert**.
4. In the **Object** dialog box, check **Display as icon** if you only want to display the PDF icon in your document. Leave it unchecked to display the first page of the PDF.
5. Click **OK**.

Double-click the PDF object in your document to open and view it in your default PDF reader.

More options

- If you just want to reuse some text from a PDF, for example a short passage, try copying and pasting it. Usually, you'll get plain text without the formatting.
- With the new PDF reflow feature in Word 2013 you can open and edit PDF content, such as paragraphs, lists and tables, just like familiar Word documents. Word pulls the content from the fixed-format PDF document and flows that content into a .docx file while preserving as much of the layout information as it can. See Edit PDF content in Word to learn more.

Appendix G

Assignment Sheet for Assignment #2: Annotated Bibliography

ASSIGNMENT #2: ANNOTATED BIBLIOGRAPHY

Length: *Each* annotation should be about 100 words in length

In-process document due date: {date}

Source Requirement: The finished project will have fifteen sources

Final Due Date: {date}

The in-process document should have at least completed eight entries

The annotated bibliography is a piece of writing that documents your research process. The purpose of an annotated bibliography is to keep track of the sources that you're encountering in your research and each piece's usefulness to your project. You won't always know if you're going to use the information you've found, but you want to be able to return to it if you do decide you want to integrate the source.

What is an annotated bibliography? A bibliography is simply a list of the sources that you've encountered while researching your subject. It's a list of the "content building" sources that you use to learn about and understand your topic. When you create an annotated bibliography, you will create a formal APA source entry and then note what is useful about the source. There are many ways to go about this, but for this class, we will use this format: a brief summary of the content of the source with a brief statement indicating how the information might fit into your MRP. The goal is to give the reader a snapshot of what the source is about and to point the reader to where they might find the information used within your larger project.

Example:

Grierson, S.T. (1999). Circling through text: Teaching research through multigenre writing. *The English Journal, 89*(1). 51–55. Retrieved from http://www.ncte.org/journals/ej

A strong overview of what a multigenre project is and how to develop a MRP for a basic writing course. Grierson gives very specific directions of how to implement the project and gives numerous specific examples of what student work might look like. He does not offer help on assessment of MRPs. This might work well in section 3, when describing the pedagogy for integrating the project.

You do not need to use all the sources from the annotated bibliography within the formal MGRP. However, if you do, you have three options for in-text citations (unless otherwise specified in the assignment sheet):

1. Use in-text, or direct, references to your sources
2. Use parenthetical, or indirect, citations to give credit to your sources
3. Use footnotes to give credit to your sources

Why are there two due dates? The first due date is to help you keep on top of your research. It's also to allow me time to review your research for possible problems that could compromise the integrity of your project.

For help with APA citations or other documentation questions, please see the APA module in D2L, refer to your writing handbook, or ask me.

Appendix H

Assignment Sheet for Assignment #3: Self-Reflection

ASSIGNMENT #3: REFLECTION AND SELF-ASSESSMENT

Due: {date}

This assignment is separate from the formal MGRP and will not count toward the minimum word count or the five required pieces of writing. Please submit digitally and retain a hardcopy for the process folder

Answer the following questions regarding your project. Each response should be about 150 words long.

1. Identify the strongest piece of writing in your multigenre project and explain why.
2. Identify the weakest piece and explain why.
3. What have you learned so far about writing in different genres?
4. What has been most surprising for you in the process of researching and creating the multigenre research project?

Appendix I

Final Workshop for MGRP Self-Contained Unit

Checklist for Final Workshop Day:

- € Total word count exceeds 2,500 (total word count is: _____)
- € Five pieces of writing are included (total number of pieces is: _____)
- € Four different genres are represented (list each used:
  _____
  _____
  _____)
- € Seven sources within the overall project are cited using (Author, date) and page number when applicable.
- € Title Page includes Title, Name, Date, and Class
- € Table of Contents lists all pieces by title of piece (and not by genre)
- € Each piece of writing has a Bibliography with at least two sources listed in formal APA format
- € Piece #1 has a formal References page with matching in-text citations

How to assemble the final project for submission:

- Copy and paste all the pieces into a new Word document (save first as Final MGRP_LastName)
- Turn non-digital files into .pdf, .jpeg, or .tif files. Insert these into separate Word documents for integration into the final document.
- Be sure the final project has all the required pieces included: Title page, table of contents, at least five pieces of writing representing at least four different genres (including a formal Annotated Bibliography).
- Once everything is in one big document, insert page numbers.
- Once page numbers have been inserted, double check the table of contents to make sure it matches up.
- Create a running header along the upper right header: "Multigenre Research Project Final: {last name}"
- Save to the folder titled "Multigenre Research Project Final"

Ask for help in inserting page numbers, page breaks, or orientation of pages in Word documents.

Rotate a page to landscape or portrait orientation

You can choose either portrait (vertical) or landscape (horizontal) orientation for all or part of your document.

Change the orientation of your entire document

1. Click > **Page Layout** > **Orientation**.

2. Click **Portrait** or **Landscape**.

Note When you change the orientation, the cover pages in the Cover Page gallery change to the orientation you've chosen.

Use different orientations in the same document

There may be times when you want certain pages or sections of your document to have a different orientation from the rest of it. Note that Word puts selected text on its own page, and the surrounding text on separate pages.

1. Select the pages or paragraphs whose orientation you want to change.
2. Click **Page Layout** > **Page Setup** Dialog Box Launcher.

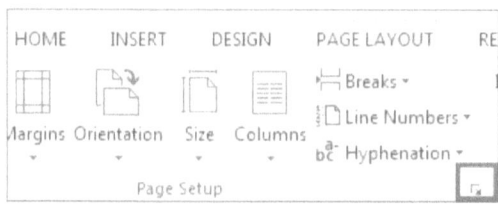

1. In the **Page Setup** box, under **Orientation**, click **Portrait** or **Landscape**.

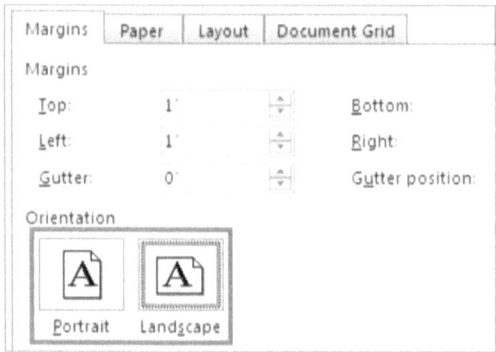

1. Click the **Apply to** box and click **Selected text**.

Appendix I 119

Note Word automatically inserts section breaks before and after the text that has the new page orientation. If your document is already divided into sections, you can click in a section (or select multiple sections), and then change the orientation for only the sections that you select. Read about how to find out where the section breaks are in your document.

Add a PDF to a document

You can insert a PDF into a Word document as an object that you can open and view. You'll be able to re-size it, but you can't edit it.

1. Click **Insert > Object**.

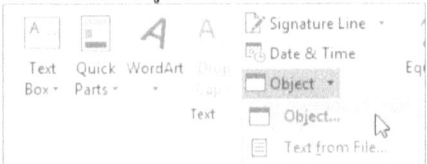

2. In the **Object** dialog box, click **Create from File** and then click **Browse**.
3. Find the PDF you want to insert, and then click **Insert**.
4. In the **Object** dialog box, check **Display as icon** if you only want to display the PDF icon in your document. Leave it unchecked to display the first page of the PDF.
5. Click **OK**.

Double-click the PDF object in your document to open and view it in your default PDF reader.

More options

- If you just want to reuse some text from a PDF, for example a short passage, try copying and pasting it. Usually, you'll get plain text without the formatting.
- With the new PDF reflow feature in Word 2013 you can open and edit PDF content, such as paragraphs, lists and tables, just like familiar Word documents. Word pulls the content from the fixed-format PDF document and flows that content into a .docx file while preserving as much of the layout information as it can. See Edit PDF content in Word to learn more.

Appendix J

List of Former Student Topics

The following are a sampling of topics that students have used in our classes from 2007 to 2015.

101st Airborne Division in the Battle of the Bulge
Alcoholism
Aldo Leopold
Allyson Felix
Andrew McMahon (musician)
Anne Frank
Anorexia Nervosa
Applying to Veterinarian School
Automobiles and their charitable associations
Baseball
Basketball
Battle of Berlin
Bin Laden and Adolf Hitler
Blackmill Dance
Bobby Orr
Caffeine Effects
Cancer
Capuchin Monkeys
Cars: Not Just a Hobby
Cartooning
Challenges of Blind People
Chris McCandless
Cirque De Soleil
Climate Change
Coffee
Computers and Technology
Conspiracy Theories
Dave Schultz, Olympic Wrestler
D-Day of WWII
Derek Jeter
Disney Parks
Eating Disorders
Eating Healthy
Electric Guitars
Evolution vs. Creationism
Eye Color Genetics
Fostering Kids
Frank McCourt
Free Weights and Resistance Machines
French Revolution
Gender Roles
Genetically Modified Foods
George W. Bush's approval ratings
Harley Davison
Heart of Darkness

History of Ford Cars
Illegal Immigration in America
ISIS
Jack Nicklaus
Joe Mauer
Lady Gaga
Lauren Carlini
League of Legends
Lean Manufacturing
LeBron James
Longboarding
March of Dimes
Marilyn Monroe
Medicinal Marijuana
Medieval Times
Michael Jordan
Minnesota Wild
Music of the 1960s
Muslims in America
NASCAR
Navy SEALS
Neil Patrick Harris
Pearl Harbor
Photography
Post-Traumatic Stress Disorder in the Modern Military
Power of Positive Thinking
Randy Moss
Rodeos

Sex Trafficking
Spartacus
Standardized Testing
Star Wars
Steroid Use in Athletes
Summer Fashion Outlook
Surfing
Quentin Tarantino
The PGA
The Titanic
The Trilateral Commission
The War in Afghanistan
Toilets
Top Teams in MLB
Transcendentalism
Trojan Horse
Veganism
Weather on 9/11
Welfare in America
Women in Engineering
Women in Science
Women's Basketball
Woodstock
Workout Addiction
World of Warcraft
Youth Gangs
Zodiac Killer
Zombies
Zoos

Appendix K

Formal Submission Expectations for MGRP Self-Contained Unit

Formal Submission Expectations

1. Digital copy of formal project submitted to learning management system by: {date}
2. Word count page assembled (separately from final submission packet)
3. Cover—can be anything you want, but at minimum it should contain your name, the title of the project, the class it is submitted for, and the date
4. Table of Contents (strongly recommended: you can omit this if you want, but it might be helpful in seeing the overall unity of the project)
5. Required Writing Piece #1: Background, overview, summary—research-based writing with formal in-text citations and a formal References at end
6. Required Writing Piece #2: The annotated bibliography. I suggest including this as the last piece of the project, but you can determine where it best fits in your project. Be sure to adhere to the formal requirements of APA formatting and style.
7. Other Required Pieces of Writing
   a. Each piece should have a clear title—be as descriptive in your title as appropriate. Use a header in lieu of a title for any genres that don't typically have a titles
   b. Each piece needs to include a bibliography or references, whichever is more appropriate for the documentation style and genre chosen
   c. Order the pieces to match the table of contents
   d. Create digital copies of handwritten/drawn pieces
8. Endnotes page (if necessary)
9. Annotated bibliography: this will be in formal APA documentation style.

On submission day, you will turn in the hard copy of your final project as well as the "research process" folder of all prewriting, drafting, revising, etc. so that if questions emerge as to the integrity of the writing or the research, there will be a wealth of documentation to fall on for evidence and support.

How to document your sources in the multigenre research paper

Piece 1: Assignment #1—you will use formal APA in-text parenthetical citations with a formal References page attached. This is essentially a mini-research-based essay.

ASSIGNMENT #2: ANNOTATED BIBLIOGRAPHY WILL ADHERE TO FORMAL APA STYLE

Additional Pieces:

- All direct quotes will be documented with the author (date) style. A bibliography will be attached to each piece, regardless of whether the genre would require one or not.
- Pictures, maps, and other images will be documented according to APA with the caption appearing under or beside the borrowed image.
- Information that is not specific to a source but that has emerged from your research of the subject will not be formally cited in these pieces, but the sources must appear in a bibliography. You can choose to have the bibliography attached to the piece as a small textbox somewhere in the page or as a separate page that is immediately after the piece it is referring to.

Appendix L

MGRP Grading Rubric for Whole Semester Assignment

Quality and use of research
Quite simply, what kind of sources have you used and how effectively have you used them? How does the research add to your project? Is it integrated effectively?

/ 35

Organization, development, structure
How does the information translate on the page? Is it structured in a sensible way? Is there a logical progression from point to point? Are each of the points of the writing developed fully or are there gaping holes that need to be filled?

/ 40

Grammar and mechanics
Spelling, mechanics, grammar, you probably know the drill by now.

/ 15

Creativity
Yes . . . I realize this is rather arbitrary, ambiguous, and subjective, but creativity is important here as well. Are there obvious signs that you're not "phoning it in," and actually going "above and beyond" the basic rote requirements of the assignment? If so, you'll do well.

/ 10

Total: / 100 ()

Appendix M

MGRP Grading Rubric for Self-Contained Unit

MGRP Grading Rubric for Self-Contained Unit.

Criteria	Score	Excellent to Very Good (25–22)	Good to Average (21–18)	Weak (17–11)	Failing (10–5)
Focus and organization (25)		• Project has one unified focus • Pieces of writing are ordered in a logical way • A variety of genres are represented • Relationship between each piece of writing/genre is clear and purposeful • Each piece of writing adheres to the rules of the genre it is representing	• Project has a focus, but it isn't unified for all the content. • Some logical ordering of pieces of writing is missing • Writer has limited representation of genres • Relationship between pieces of writing is adequate • Not all pieces of writing adhere to the genre form they are representing	• Overall unity of project is tenuous • Logical ordering of pieces of writing is weak • Writer has underrepresentation of genres • Relationships between pieces of writing is weak • General misuse of genre forms	• Project lacks one focus/no unity • No logical ordering of pieces of writing • Writer has underrepresentation of genres • No relationship evident between pieces of writing or genres • Genre forms are not adhered to correctly
Content (25)		• Each piece of writing is fully developed: Information is interesting and contains depth of information expected for an academic audience • Content is clearly based on quality research • There is limited dependence on opinion/previous knowledge	• Most pieces of writing are fully developed: Information is mostly suitable for an academic audience • Content is mostly based on quality research • There is limited dependence on opinion/previous knowledge	• Some pieces of writing are not fully developed: Information is superficial or too general for an academic audience • Content is based on questionable sources/research • Depends too heavily on opinion/previous knowledge	• Notable lack of development in numerous pieces of writing; Information is neither new nor engaging • Content is based on poor research/sources • Depends mostly on opinion/previous knowledge

Appendix M

Criteria	(Excellent)	(Good)	(Fair)	(Poor)
Use of sources (25)	• Appropriate sources chosen and integrated into every piece of writing • Sources' ideas are well-understood • Summaries and paraphrases fully developed • Quotations used selectively and explained clearly • Each piece of writing has a Bibliography or References page • Appropriate documentation used for specific genres	• Adequate sources chosen and integrated into most pieces of writing • Sources' ideas understood on a basic level but lack depth • Summaries and paraphrases are adequately developed • Quotations generally suitable, though some may be inappropriately selected, inadequately discussed, or overused • Each piece of writing has a Bibliography or References page • Some errors in documentation choices for genres	• Writer exhibits poor quality of sources; source material not integrated carefully into writing • Sources' ideas discussed but misunderstood or plagiarized • Summaries and paraphrases are not fully developed • Quotations absent or overused and under-explained • Some pieces of writing lack a Bibliography or a References page • Numerous errors in documentation choices for different genres	• Overall poor choice of sources for content • Sources referenced but not explained • General lack of sources used • Plagiarism a significant problem in summaries and paraphrases • Relies too heavily on direct quotations • No significant effort made to include a Bibliography or a list of References • Prolific errors in documentation of sources/lack of understanding for inclusion of sources in different genres
Grammar, syntax, mechanics, in-text citation, Documentation, formatting (15%)	• Sentence-level errors limited • All source material is clearly credited to its source using APA style • References/Bibliographies are APA compliant	• Sentence-level errors generally managed but may begin to diminish clarity • Most source material is clearly credited to its source using APA style • References/Bibliographies have APA formatting issues	• Sentence-level errors frequent and inhibit understanding • APA: Borrowed material not clearly marked • References/Bibliographies doesn't adhere to APA requirements	• Sentence-level errors dominate the essay • No visible attempt to integrate sources with author/quote • References/Bibliographies are noncompliant • Borrowed material missing documentation
Creativity (10%)	• Project displays outstanding intellectual creativity in connections made • Project displays excellent aesthetic creativity in the presentation of research/content	• Project displays good intellectual creativity in connections made • Project displays good aesthetic creativity in the presentation of research/content	• Project attempts to display intellectual creativity in connections made • Project attempts to display aesthetic creativity in the presentation of research/content	• Project lacks intellectual creativity in connections made • Project lacks aesthetic creativity in the presentation of research/content
Total (100%)				

Appendix N

List of Potential Genres

Students can use a variety of genres for the MGRP. However, it's important that all of the genres chosen are writing-based genres that reinforce the core writing skills of the course. This is not an all-inclusive list, but it's helpful for students if you can provide them a list to get their minds moving in the direction of using different genres.

Students will often venture away from this list, which is great! The important thing is simply that the students learn to investigate how to use various genres and how to write within the specific parameters of the genres they choose to use. Additionally, it's useful to reiterate at various times in the unit the importance of the unity of the finished project.

Advertisements	Children's books	Eulogies
Advice columns	Class notes	Facebook entries
Sports trading cards	Contracts	Fairy tales
Biographies	Crossword puzzles	Family trees
Birth announcements	Daily schedules	Graffiti
Book jackets	Dedications	Greeting cards
Bottle labels	Definitions	Historical fiction
Brochures	Dialogues	Horoscopes
Bulletins	Diaries	Instructions
Bumper stickers	Diplomas	Interviews
Calendars	Directions	Invitations
Campaign speeches	Driver's license	Journal entries
Cards	Editorials	Laboratory notes
Cartoons/comic strips	Email messages	Leases
Catalogs	Encyclopedia entries	Letters
CD liners	Epitaphs	Magazine articles

Magazine covers
Manifestos
Maps
Medical records
Membership cards
Memos
Menus
Myths
News releases
Newscasts
Obituaries
Pamphlets
Parodies

Parodies
Personal data/favorite
Play/skit
Poems
Police reports
Postcards
Prayers
Psychiatrists' reports
Questionnaires
Radio show transcripts
Recipes
Requisitions
Resumes

Schedules
Shopping lists
Song lyrics
Speeches
Surveys
Telegrams
Telephone conversations
Textbook sections
Tickets
Timelines
Twitter conversations
Wanted posters
Wills

Bibliography

Allen, C. A. (2001). *Multigenre research paper: Voice, passion, and discovery in grades 4–6.* Portsmouth, NH: Heinemann.

Allen, C. A., & Swistak, L. (2004, January). Multigenre research: The power of choice and interpretation. *Language Arts*, 81(3), 223–232. Retrieved from http://www.ncte.org/journals.

Autrey, K. (1991, Autumn). Toward a rhetoric of journal writing. *Rhetoric Review*, 10(1), 74–90. doi:10.1080/07350199109388952.

Bailey, N. M., & Carroll, K. M. (2010, July). Motivating students' research skills and interests through a multimodal, multigenre research project. *The English Journal*, 99(6), 78–85. doi:10.2307/20787674.

Bazerman, C. (2007). Genres and cognitive development: Beyond writing to learn. In *Genre in a Changing World.* (pp. 279–294). Retrieved from http://wac.colostate.edu/books/genre/.

Belanoff, P., & Dickson, M. (Eds.). (1991) *Portfolios: Process and product.* Portsmouth, NH: Boynton/Cook Publishers.

Bowen, B. (1991, April). A multi-genre approach to the art of the biographer. *The English Journal*, 80(4), 53–54. doi:10.2307/819166.

Broad, B. (2003). *What we really value: Beyond rubrics in teaching and assessing writing.* Logan, UT: Utah State University Press.

Cate, T. (2000). "This is cool!" Multigenre research reports. *The Social Studies*, 91(3), 137–140. doi: 10.1080/00377990009602457.

Damiani, V. B. (2004). Portfolio assessment in the classroom. *Helping Children at Home and School II.* Bethesda, MD: National Association of School Psychologists.

Daniell, B., Davis, L., Stewart, L., & Tabor, E. (2008, Fall). The in-house conference: A strategy for disrupting order and shifting identities. *Pedagogy*, 8(3), 447–465. doi:10.1215/15314200–2008-005.

Davis, R., & Shadle, M. (2000, February). "Building a mystery": Alternative research writing and the academic act of seeking. *College Composition and Communication*, 51(3), 417–446. doi:10.2307/358743.

Denney, M., Grier, J. M., & Buchanan, M. (2012, August). Establishing a portfolio assessment framework for pre-service teachers: A multiple perspectives approach. *Teaching in Higher Education*, 17(4), 425–437. doi:10.1080/13562517.2011.640997.

Dickson, R., DeGraff, J., & Foard, M. (2002, November). Learning about self and others through multigenre research projects. *The English Journal*, 92(2), 82–90. doi: 10.2307/822230.

Doubleday, J. F. (1984, September). The "research paper" in the writing course: A comment. *College English*, 46(5), 512–513. doi:10.2307/377061.

Doyle, P. (2013). *World War II in numbers: An infographic guide to the conflict, Its conduct, and Its casualties*. Richmond Hill, Ontario: Firefly Books Ltd.

Duke, N. K., Caughlan, S., Juzwik, M. M., & Martin, N. M. (2012). *Reading and writing genre with purpose*. Portsmouth, NH: Heinemann.

Dunn, J.S., Jr, Luke, C., & Nassar, D. (2013). Valuing the resources of infrastructure: Beyond from-scratch and off-the-shelf technology options for electronic portfolio assessment in first-year writing. *Computers and Composition*, 30, 61–73. doi:10.1016/j.compcom.2012.12.001.

Edminster, J., & Moxley, J. (2002). Graduate education and the evolving genre of electronic theses and dissertations. *Computers and Composition*, 19, 89–104. doi:10.1016/S8755–4615(02)00082–8.

Flurkey, A. D., & Goodman, Y. M. (2004, January). The role of genre in a text: Reading through the waterworks. *Language Arts*, 81(3), 233–244. Retrieved from http://www.ncte.org/journals.

Gillespie, J. (2005, May). "It would be fun to do again": Multigenre responses to literature. *Journal of Adolescent & Adult Literacy*, 48(8), 678–684. doi:10.1598/JAAL.48.8.5.

Gillis, C. (2002, November). Multiple voices, multiple genres: Fiction for young adults. *The English Journal*, 92(2), 52–59. doi:10.2307/822226.

Goldfinch, E. (2003, April/May). A match made in heaven: The multigenre project marries imagination and research skills. *Library Media Connection*, 21(7), 26–28. Retrieved from http://www.abc-clio.com/.

Grierson, S. T. (1999, September). Circling through text: Teaching research through multigenre writing. *The English Journal*, 89(1), 51–55. doi: 10.2307/821356.

Hicks, T. (2013). *Crafting digital writing: Composing texts across media and genres*. Portsmouth, NH: Heinemann.

Hughes, H. (2009, March). Multigenre research projects. *Middle School Journal*, 40(4), 34–43. doi:10.1080/00940771.2009.11461679.

Huot, B. (2002). *(Re)articulating writing assessment for teaching and learning*. Logan, UT: Utah State University Press.

Huot, B., & O'Neill, P. (2009). *Assessing writing: A critical sourcebook*. Boston: Bedford/St. Martin's.

Johnson, S. A. (2007). *Old words in new orders: Multigenre essays in the composition Classroom*. University of Massachusetts.

Kiley, K. (2011, April). No room for books. *Inside Higher Ed*. Retrieved from https://wwwlinsidehighered.com.

Kolowich, S. (2011). What students don't know. *Inside Higher Ed*. Retrieved from https://www.insidehighered.com.

Lam, R. (2013, November). Promoting self-regulated learning through portfolio assessment: Testimony and recommendations. *Assessment & Evaluation in Higher Education*, 39(6), 699–714. doi:10.1080/02602938.2013.862211.

Lankow, J., Ritchie, J., & Crooks, R. (2012). *Infographics: The power of visual storytelling*. Hoboken, NJ: Wiley.

Larson, R. L. (2002, November). The "research paper" in the writing course: A non-form of writing. *College English,* 44(8), 811–816. doi: 10.2307/822230.

LeNoir, W. D. (2002, November). The multigenre warning label. *The English Journal,* 92(2), 99–101. doi: 10.2307/822232.

Lowood, J. (2013, November/December). Restructuring the writing program at Berkeley city college: Or how we learned to love assessment and use it to improve student learning. *Assessment Update,* 25(6), 6–14. doi:10.1002/au.

Lynne, P. (2004). *Coming to terms: A theory of writing assessment*. Logan, UT: Utah State University Press.

MacBride, M. (2017). Breaking the ice: The teacher as "story." Fulton, A., Field, C., & MacBride M. (Eds.), *Tell me a story: Using narratives to break down barriers in composition courses*. Lanham, MD: Rowman & Littlefield.

Mack, N. (2002, November). The ins, outs, and in-betweens of multigenre writing. *English Journal* 92(2), 91–98. doi:10.2307/822231.

Mack, N. (2006). Ethical representation of working-class lives: Multiple genres, voices, and identities. *Pedagogy,* 6(1), 53–78. doi:10.1215/15314200-6-1-53.

Mack, N. (2013). Multigenre report writing: Teaching handouts. *Dr. Nancy Mack.* Retrieved from http://www.wright.edu/~nancy.mack/mghandouts.htm.

Mack, N. (2015). *Engaging writers with multigenre research projects: A teacher's guide*. New York: Teachers College Press.

McClelland, K. (1991). Portfolios: Solution to a problem. In P. Belanoff & M. Dickson (Eds.), *Portfolios: Process and product* (pp. 165–173). Portsmouth, NH: Heinemann.

McClure, H. and Toth, C. (2015). Louder than words: Using infographics to teach the value of information and authority. In P. Bravender, H. A. McClure, & G. Schaub (Eds.), *Teaching information literacy threshold concepts: Lesson plans for librarians* (pp. 166–172). Chicago, IL: Association of College and Research Libraries.

Moulton, M. R. (1999, April). The multigenre paper: Increasing interest, motivation, and functionality in research. *Journal of Adolescent & Adult Literacy,* 42(7), 528–539. Retrieved from http://onlinelibrary.wiley.com/.

Moynihan, K. E. (2007, September). A collectibles project: Engaging students in authentic multimodal research and writing. *The English Journal*, 97(1), 69–76. doi:10.2307/30047211.

Murray, R., Shea, M., & Shea, B. (2004, Fall). Avoiding the one-size-fits-all curriculum: Textsets, inquiry, and differentiating instruction. *Childhood Education,* 81(1), 33–35. doi:10.1080/00094056.2004.10521291.

Painter, D. D. (2009, May). Providing differentiated learning experiences through multigenre projects. *Invention in School and Clinic,* 44(5), 288–293. doi:10.1177/1053451208330900.

Paré, A., Starke-Meyerring, D., & McAlpine, L. (2006). The dissertation as multi-genre: Many readers, many readings. In *Genre in a changing world* (pp. 179–193). Retrieved from http://wac.colostate.edu/books/genre/chapter9.pdf.

Paretti, M. C., & Powell, K. M. (2009). *Assessment of writing* (Vol. 4). Tallahassee, FL: Association for Institutional Research.

Perryman-Clark, S. M. (2012, Spring). Africanized patterns of expression: A case study of African American students' expository writing patterns across written contexts. *Pedagogy,* 12(2), 253–280. doi:10.1215/15314200–1503586.

Pirie, B. (1997). *Reshaping high school English.* United States: National Council of Teachers of English.

Putz, M. (2006). *A teacher's guide to the multigenre research project.* Portsmouth, NH: Heinemann.

Quinn, T. (2013). *On grades and grading.* Lanham, MD: Rowman & Littlefield.

Qvortrup, A., & Keiding, T. B. (2015). Portfolio assessment: Production and reduction of complexity. *Assessment & Evaluation in Higher Education,* 40(3), 407–419. doi:10.1080/02602938.2014.918087.

Richison, J., Hernandez, A. C., & Carter, M. (2002, November). Blending multiple genres in theme baskets. *English Journal,* 92(2),76–81. doi:10.2307/822229.

Romano, T. (1987). Making the grade in evaluation: Keep students writing. *Clearing the way: Working with teenage writers* (pp. 107–129). Portsmouth, NH: Heinemann.

Romano, T. (1995). *Writing with passion: Life stories, multiple genres.* Portsmouth, NH: Boynton & Cook.

Romano, T. (2000). *Blending genre, altering style.* Portsmouth, NH: Heinemann.

Romano, T. (2002). Teaching writing through multigenre papers. In R. Tremmel & W. Broz (Eds.), *Teaching writing teachers of high school and first year composition* (pp. 52–65). Portsmouth, NH: Boynton/Cook Pub.

Romano, T. (2004, March 8). The multigenre paper. *Teachers College of Columbia University.* Retrieved from http://www.tc.columbia.edu/centers/mssc/Downloads/The%20Multigenre%20Paper.doc.

Romano, T. (2013). *Fearless writing: Multigenre to motivate and inspire.* Portsmouth, NH: Heinemann.

Ruggieri, C. A. (2002, November). Multigenre, multiple intelligences, and transcendentalism. *The English Journal,* 92(2), 60–68. doi:10.2307/822227.

Selfe, C. L. (2007). *Multimodal composition: Resources for teachers.* Cresskill, NJ: Hampton Press.

Shipka, J. (2005, December). A multimodal task-based framework for composing. *College Composition and Communication,* 57(2), 277–307. Retrieved from http://www.ncte.org/journals.

Simon, L. (2007, January). Expanding literacies: Teachers' inquiry research and multigenre texts. *English Education,* 39(2), 146–176. doi:10.1080/08824099709388671.

Smith, D. J. (2014). *If. . . A mind-bending way of looking at big ideas and numbers.* Tonawnda, NY: Kids Can Press Ltd.

Styslinger, M. E. (2006, March). Multigenre-multigendered research papers. *The English Journal,* 95(4), 53–57. doi:10.2307/30047089.

Tardy, C. M. (2005). Expressions of disciplinarity and individuality in a multimodal genre. *Computers and Composition,* 22, 319–336. doi:10.1016/j.compcom.2005.05.004.

Townsend, M. A. (2001). Writing intensive courses and WAC. In S. H. McLeod, E. Miraglia, M. Soven, & C. Thaiss (Eds.), *WAC for the new millennium: Strategies for continuing WAC programs* (pp. 233–258). Urbana, IL: NCTE.

Trimbur, J. (1987, Spring). Beyond cognition: The voices in inner speech. *Rhetoric Review,* 5(2), 211–221. doi:10.1080/07350198709359146.

Wilson, M. (2006). *Rethinking rubrics in writing assessment.* Portsmouth, NH: Neinemann.

Wolfe, P. (2010, July). Preservice teachers planning for critical literacy teaching. *English Education,* 42(4), 368–390. doi:10.1353/hsj.2003.0018.

Yancey, K. B. (2001). Digitized student portfolios. In B. Cambridge (Ed.), *Electronic portfolios: Emerging practices in student, faculty, and institutional learning* (pp. 15–30). Washington, DC: American Association for Higher Education.

Youngs, S., & Barone, D. (2007). *Writing without boundaries: What's possible when students combine genres.* Portsmouth, NH: Heinemann.

Zappen, J. P., Gurak, L. J., & Doheny-Farina, S. (1997, Spring). Rhetoric, community, and cyberspace *rhetoric review,* 15(2), 400–419. doi:10.1080/07350199709359226.

Index

Allen, Camille A., 84, 85, 86, 87
analysis:
    of audience, 60;
    of genre, 57;
    of writing, 51;
    of sources. *See* research
annotated bibliography, 22–25, 41, 88, 97, 98, 102, 123;
    assignment sheet, 113–14;
    compiling, 27–28, 31–32, 37n9, 43, 113–14, 124;
    purpose of, 23, 29, 49, 91;
    as a research methodology, 32, 78, 85–87
Aristotle, 2, 16
assessment and evaluation, 8, 12, 13, 26, 32, 35–36, 49, 83–96;
    portfolio approach, 88–90;
    rubric approach, 90–95;
    self-assessment by students, 13, 46, 48, 115
audience, 11, 15–17, 22–23, 25, 30, 44, 46, 65, 94, 128;
    audience awareness activity, 60–62, 66–67;
    target audience, 57–58, 60–61

Bazerman, Charles, 3, 37n5
Belanoff, Pat, 88

best practice(s), 53n2, 83, 86, 90
Bowen, Barbara, 85
Broad, Bob, 89, 90

Carter, Marcia, 87
Cate, Timothy, 6, 8, 24
core objectives, 4, 13, 23, 84, 95;
    first-year composition curriculums, 5, 8, 17, 22, 23, 39, 93, 94
Currency, Reliability, Authorship, Accuracy, Purpose (CRAAP), 63–65
creativity, 24–25, 33, 35, 43, 46, 52, 66, 71–72, 83–85, 92;
    aesthetic creativity, 95;
    assessment of, 95, 125, 129;
    intellectual creativity, 85, 92, 95
critical thinking, 1, 8, 33, 35, 63, 71, 80
critical reading skills, 7, 41, 51–52, 81
Crooks, Ross, 72

Davis, Robert, 3, 8
DeGraff, Jon, 2, 3, 6, 8, 24, 25, 33, 34
Desire2Learn. *See* learning management systems
Dickson, Randi, 2, 3, 6, 8, 24, 25, 33, 34
Dickson, Marcia, 88
documentation. *See* annotated bibliography; research

Doyle, Peter, 73

evaluation. *See* assessment

fiction, 24, 25, 41, 50, 51, 55, 131
Foard, Mark, 2, 3, 6, 8, 24, 25, 33, 34

genre, ix, x, 3, 4, 7, 8, 13, 16, 25, 33,
    41, 51–52, 83–84, 93, 95;
    analyzing, 10, 11, 17, 20, 27, 28, 44,
        46, 49, 57–58;
    identifying, 7, 8, 28, 34, 42–43, 131;
    teaching about, 19, 21–23, 29, 37n3,
        37n5, 55–56, 66–67, 85, 87
grade sheet. *See* rubrics
Grierson, Sirpa, 6, 7, 24, 83, 84, 87, 114

Hernandez, Anita, 87
"How to" essay. *See* process essay
Huot, Brian, 89

infographics, 71–73
informal surveys, 130, 132
informative essay, 17, 18, 22, 23, 37n7

Keiding, Tina, 89
Kiley, Kevin, 30
Kolowich, Steve, 2

Lam, Ricky, 89
Lankow, Jason, 72
Larson, Richard, 2–6, 19, 37n1
Learning Management Systems, 35,
    37n5, 69, 77, 123
LeNoir, W. David, 8, 85
Library of Congress classification
    system, 31
Lynne, Patricia, 90

Mack, Nancy, 53n3, 84
McAlpine, Lynn, 8
McClelland, Kathy, 88
McClure, Hazel, 72
Moulton, Margaret, 83, 85, 86, 87
Murry, Rosemary, 86

National Council of Teachers of English
    (NCTE), 7

online research, 2, 4, 10, 18, 30, 32;
    databases, 31, 77–79;
    documentation of. *See* research;
    websites, 63–65

Paré, Anthony, 8
Paretti, Marie, 90
peer review, 25–26, 44–47
peer-sharing, 24, 26, 34–35, 44, 45, 46,
    72
Pirie, Bruce, 2
portfolios, 83–84, 87–90
Powell, Katrina, 90
presentations, 6, 35–36, 38n12, 40, 48
prewriting and drafts, 12, 16, 26, 30, 46,
    69, 89, 90, 124
process essay, 52, 68–70
process folders, 26, 31–32, 35, 47
Putz, Melinda, 83, 85, 86, 88

Quinn, Timothy, 89
Qvortrup, Ane, 89

reflection, 86, 87, 88, 89, 94.
    See also assessment
reflective writing, 21, 86
research, 1–2, 13, 19–20, 23, 25, 40, 47,
    50, 66, 71, 85, 87, 91, 93–94;
    books for research, 30–31;
    definition of, x, 3, 5, 10, 24, 33;
    Digital Public Library, 32;
    evaluating sources, 17, 63–65, 94;
    formal documentation of, 1, 12, 18,
        23, 28, 29, 40, 41, 45, 46, 85, 86,
        87, 98, 124, 129;
    Google books, 31–32;
    Google Scholar, 32;
    library research, 18, 30–32, 74–75,
        77–78;
    methods of, xi, 2, 6, 18, 27, 45, 86,
        94;
    purpose of, 2–3

research-based essay, 3, 5–8, 18, 10, 19, 20, 22, 24, 34, 39, 85, 94, 124
response essay, 17, 18
resume(s), 4, 20, 22, 132
reverse outline, 49
rhetorical situation, 7, 8, 11, 15, 16, 17, 18, 22, 34, 52, 57, 66
Ritchie, Josh, 72
Richison, Jeanine, 87
Romano, Tom, ix, 6, 7, 10, 24, 33, 50, 83, 84, 85, 86, 87
rubrics, 83–84, 86, 89, 95

Science, Technology, Engineering, Art, and Math (STEAM), 4
Shadle, Mark, 3, 8
Shea, Brian, 86
Shea, Mary, 86
Smith, David, 73
Starke-Meyerring, Doreen, 8
student reflections. *See* assessment; reflection; reflective writing
summary, 18, 22, 23, 26, 28, 46–47, 58, 71, 80–81, 86, 98, 105, 107
synthesis essay, 3, 85
synthesizing sources, 17, 18, 85

thesis statements, 15, 18, 40, 45
topic selection, 10–11, 20–22, 23, 25–26, 27, 29, 30, 37n4, 43–47, 74, 88, 92, 99, 101;
list of former student topics, 121
Toth, Christopher, 72
Townsend, Martha, 39, 53n2

unity in writing, 16, 20, 28, 67, 85, 86, 93

voice in student writing, 6, 8, 13, 21, 33, 34

web sources. *See* Currency, Reliability, Authorship, Accuracy, Purpose (CRAAP); research
Writing Across the Curriculum (WAC), 4
workshop, 25–26, 28–35, 46
writing process. *See* brainstorming; prewriting and drafts; process folders
Writing Program Administrators (WPA), 7
writing with purpose, 15–16

Yancey, Kathleen, 86, 88, 89

About the Authors

Heidi Wall Burns earned an MA in English from Iowa State University, and a double BA in English and Spanish from Dickinson State University. She has taught introductory courses in first-year composition, literature, and speech at a variety of intuitions, including a large research institution, a rural-based community college, an inner-city community college, an e-campus for a large urban community college, and a mid-sized traditional four-year institution. Each of these experiences has reinforced her belief that writing pedagogy needs to continually evolve to meet the unprecedented writing needs of today's students.

Heidi's belief that the current methodology used in first-year composition classrooms is inadequate is what led her to create the study on which this book is founded. In addition, she has published several articles on teaching, as well as presented at regional and national conferences. Her goal is to encourage other instructors to take risks in their classrooms and to continue offering more effective learning opportunities for students. In spring 2016, she was awarded the contingent faculty award from her current institution for her innovation in the classroom.

When she's not busy grading or dreaming up new ideas to use in the classroom, Heidi also works as an independent editor. She has worked on over a hundred titles, from juvenile literature to doctoral dissertations, in all phases from concept to final proofing. She can be reached at pipburns@gmail.com, via LinkedIn at Heidi Burns, or on Twitter @BurnsPippy.

Michael MacBride received his PhD in English from Southern Illinois University, Carbondale, in 2014, his MA in literature from Minnesota State University, Mankato, and his BS in creative writing from Eastern Michigan

University. Since 2005, he has taught a variety of English, literature, and humanities courses at six different institutions.

Although his primary area of research is nineteenth-century American literature, he has additional expertise in contemporary American literature, Latin American literature, rhetoric and composition, and comic studies. This balance of course work and scholarship allows him to help students make connections across centuries, cultures, and genres and become better critical readers and thinkers of the world around them. Regardless if students are in a face-to-face, online, or hybrid setting, Michael believes it is essential that students find a personal connecteion to their writing.

In addition to his teaching, Michael also regularly presents at professional conferences. Two of his favorites are NCTE and the Comics Arts Conference at the San Diego Comic Con. He can be reached via email at michael.macbride@gmail.com, on Twitter @michaelmacbride.

www.ingramcontent.com/pod-product-compliance
Lightning Source LLC
Chambersburg PA
CBHW021845220426
43663CB00005B/409